Acknowledgments

Stopping Valium is a product of the work of many people, who have given generously of time, talent, and material to focus public attention on the dangers of Valium and related drugs.

Phyllis McCarthy, Office Manager of Public Citizen Health Research Group, typed and edited the manuscript and organized the production of *Stopping Valium* from start to finish. This book would not have happened without her.

Every member of the Public Citizen Health Research Group staff participated in the preparation of *Stopping Valium,* by reading drafts, offering suggestions, supplying information, assisting with production, and performing countless other necessary tasks. They include: Henry Bergman, Benjamin Gordon, Allen Greenberg, Cynthia Grove, Cary LaCheen, Lisa Northcutt, Linda Rabinowitz, and Maggie White.

The National Institute on Drug Abuse supplied information on Community Correspondents Groups working in the field of drug addiction.

The National Consumers League, Inc. and their Legislative Director, Barbara Pequet, provided information on Valium and related drugs for use in this book.

We also thank the many people at the Drug Enforcement Agency, the Food and Drug Administration, and the National Institute on Drug Abuse who chose to remain anonymous, for their help.

In 1981 the Reagan administration allowed the FDA to suspend a rule that would have required the following to be included in every new Valium prescription, with similar warnings required for the other drugs in the same chemical family as Valium:

- "You can become dependent on Valium. Dependence is a craving for the drug or the inability to function normally without it."
- "An overdose of Valium alone or in combination with other drugs or alcohol and tranquilizers dangerously increases the effects of both."
- "You should avoid drinking alcohol while taking Valium. The combination of alcohol and tranquilizers dangerously increases the effects of both."
- "Studies suggest an increased rate of birth defects in children whose mothers took Valium during the first three months of pregnancy."
- "If you have been taking Valium for a month or more, your doctor should reassess your condition and your continued use of the drug. The effect of these drugs for the relief of anxiety for periods longer than four months has not been studied."

These are a few of the facts that you would have learned from the canceled *Patient Package Insert* (PPI) for Valium and similar drugs—facts that the drug companies have fought vigorously to keep from you; facts you should know about.

STOPPING VALIUM
and Ativan, Centrax, Dalmane, Librium, Paxipam, Restoril, Serax, Tranxene, Xanax

STOPPING VALIUM

and Ativan, Centrax, Dalmane, Librium, Paxipam, Restoril, Serax, Tranxene, Xanax

by Eve Bargmann, M.D.,
Sidney M. Wolfe, M.D.,
Joan Levin,
and the Public Citizen
Health Research Group

WARNER BOOKS

A Warner Communications Company

Warner Books Edition

This Warner Books Edition is published by arrangement with Public Citizen Health Research Group, 2000 P Street, NW, Washington, DC 20036.

Warner Books, Inc., 666 Fifth Avenue, New York, NY 10103

A Warner Communications Company

Printed in the United States of America
First Warner printing: May 1983
10 9 8 7 6 5 4 3 2 1

Library of Congress Cataloging in Publication Data
Bargmann, Eve.
Stopping valium, and ativan, centrax, dalmane,
librium, paxipam, restoril, serax, tranxene, xanax.

Reprint. Originally published: Washington, D.C.:
Public Citizen Health Research Group, c1982.
Includes index.
1. Diazepam—Toxicology. 2. Benzodiazepines—Toxicology. 3. Benzodiazepines—Safety measures.
4. Medication abuse. 5. Drug abuse—Treatment—United States—Directories. 6. Advertising—Drugs—United States. I. Wolfe, Sidney M. II. Levin, Joan.
III. Public Citizen, inc. Health Research Group.
IV. Title.
[RA1242.D44B37 1983] 362.2'9 82-20297
ISBN 0-446-37582-9 (USA)
ISBN 0-446-37648-5 (Canada)

Book design by H. Roberts Design

Contents

STOPPING VALIUM

1

Introduction

Valium is a registered trademark of Roche Products Inc. for one of several chemically similar drugs called benzodiazepines (pronounced: behn' zoh-die-ay'' zah-peen). Other benzodiazepine drugs include Ativan, Centrax, Dalmane, Librium, Paxipam, Restoril, Serax, Tranxene, and Xanax.* These benzodiazepines are manufactured by a number of different companies. Although much of the discussion in this book is about Valium, the statements are generally applicable to the other benzodiazepines as well. They are all chemical cousins to Valium, the best-known, biggest-selling benzodiazepine.

*As this book goes to press, another member of the benzodiazepine family has been approved for sale in the U.S. It is Halcion (triazalam), sold by Upjohn Company.

Each day millions of white, yellow, and blue Valium pills are pulled from American pockets, handbags, and medicine chests.

Each year from 1972 until 1980 (the last year for which reliable figures are available), Valium has been the most widely prescribed drug in the United States.

Sales of Valium and its chemical cousins, the benzodiazepines, have soared to phenomenal heights over the past 15 years, fueled by massive promotional efforts.

So successful have these campaigns been that today more than 10 million Americans are taking Valium or one of its chemical cousins. According to the Food and Drug Administration, 1.5 million people have taken these drugs long enough to be in serious danger of addiction.[1]

Addiction? Yes! Because what few people know—though the word is getting out—is that Valium and its chemical relations are not at all the safe tension-relievers the drug-company promotional wizards would have us believe.

Addiction to Valium and similar drugs is a major problem in this country. Over 8,000 emergency room visits a year result from such addiction.[2] And every year, 4,500 people enter drug-treatment centers for the first time to be treated for tranquilizer addiction.[3]

The thousands of people seeking treatment for addiction to Valium and its chemical cousins are likely to be a minority of those who are addicted. Many of the 1.5 million people who have taken Valium and similar drugs continuously for over 4 months may be addicted, but they may not know it because they have not stopped taking these drugs and therefore have not developed withdrawal symptoms. Many others have been treated by private doctors rather than by drug-treatment centers; and many who know or suspect that they are addicted may not yet have sought help.

If you told your doctor that you were anxious and he or she recommended that you treat it by drinking a pint of whiskey a day for the next six months, you would probably be shocked. Yet Valium and all benzodiazepines, like alcohol, are addicting drugs—and a prescription, especially one with refills, may give you enough to result in addiction.

Many people—including many doctors—do not realized that taking the *usually prescribed doses* of Valium and like drugs can result in addiction. Stopping Valium or any benzodiazepine abruptly after a few months or less of continuous use may result in withdrawal symptoms that range in severity from anxiety and inability to sleep to hallucinations and seizures.

Often a prescription for Valium amounts to a prescription for addiction. On the average, it contains 55 pills, enough for 20 days; in many cases, it can be refilled 5 times. This provides a 4-month supply of 330 pills—a potentially addicting dose. And just a phone call to the doctor can secure another 4 months' worth.

Addiction is just one of the dangers you face when you take Valium or any benzodiazepine. You need to know about these dangers if you take these drugs—or if you are even thinking about taking them.

Valium and the Benzodiazepine Family

Valium is the biggest seller in a very closely knit family of drugs called the benzodiazepines. They have wonderfully tranquil names: Librium, Restoril, Serax, Tranxene.

Though these drugs come in a variety of names and shapes, their effects are for all practical purposes the same. The British Committee on the Review of Medicines put it this way: "The committee found that all benzodiazepines were efficacious in the short-term treatment of symptoms of anxiety and insomnia. It found no evidence which could justify the preferential use of any particular benzodiazepine in either anxiety or insomnia."[4]

In this country, the *Medical Letter* was even more blunt: "All benzodiazepines are effective for treatment of anxiety and insomnia; calling some anti-anxiety drugs and others hypnotics (sleeping pills) has more to do with marketing than with pharmacology."[5]

Table I lists all the drugs of the Valium family available in this country as of 1982. Two of these, Dalmane and Restoril, are sold as sleeping pills*; the rest, including Valium, are sold as tranquilizers.

While all these drugs share similar actions and similar dangers and side effects, there are some differences among them. Valium belongs to a long-acting group of benzodiazepines, all of which can remain in the body for days. This group also includes Centrax, Dalmane, Librium, Paxipam, and Tranxene. Drugs in the shorter-acting group, including Ativan, Serax, Restoril, and Halcion, generally leave the body in less than a day. The shorter-acting drugs may be less likely to cause drowsiness the day after you take them and they may be less likely to accumulate to dangerous levels in older people and in people with liver disease. On the other hand, these short-acting drugs may also produce more dramatic withdrawal symptoms if dependence develops.

For the most part, all the members of the Valium family are different brands of one basic drug. To speak of the dangers of Valium is really to speak of the dangers of all these drugs.

*Halcion, the latest addition to the benzodiazepine family, is also a sleeping pill.

Table I

VALIUM AND THE BENZODIAZEPINE FAMILY

Brand Name	Generic Name	Manu-facturer	Daily Dose	Cost*
Ativan	lorazepam	Wyeth	1–10 mg	$4.07
Centrax	prazepam	Parke-Davis	20–60 mg	$3.67
Dalmane	flurazepam	Roche	15–30 mg	$2.24
Halcion	triazalam	Upjohn	0.125–0.5 mg	NA
Librium	chlordiazepoxide	Roche	15–100 mg	$4.38
Libritabs (generic forms)	chlordiazepoxide	(several)	15–100 mg	$2.19
Paxipam	halazepam	Schering	60–160 mg	NA
Restoril	temazepam	Sandoz	15–30 mg	NA
Serax	oxazepam	Wyeth	10–30 mg	$4.60
Tranxene SD, Tranxene	clorazepate	Abbott	15–60 mg	$4.37
Valium	diazepam	Roche	4–40 mg	$4.80
Xanax	alprazolam	Upjohn	0.75–4 mg	NA

*Approximate cost for an average 10-day supply
NA: Not Available

The Dangers of Valium and Its Chemical Cousins

Most people who use benzodiazepine drugs such as Valium have not been told about all of its dangers. As a matter of fact, doctors who prescribe these drugs often dismiss the risks with the assertion that, all in all, these drugs are remarkably safe.

When you purchase a drug at a pharmacy, you have not finished paying for your treatment. The costs of taking a drug include common annoying side effects, as well as the risk of more serious reactions.

A few of the costs of taking Valium and other benzodiazepines are

- **Mental impairment:** Mental and physical abilities decline measurably in the majority of people who use Valium-type drugs. Memory and learning ability become predictably worse in people who have taken these drugs. Drowsiness, decreased coordination, and slowed reaction times are other frequent effects.[6]
- **Impaired driving:** Driving skills, such as braking ability, are significantly impaired after taking Valium-like drugs.[7] People who have taken Valium or similar drugs are also more likely to have traffic accidents.[8]
- **Confusion, hallucinations, paradoxical rage:** Some people have severe mental reactions due to Valium and other benzodiazepines. These are unusual, but they are also dangerous.[9]
- **Addiction:** As already discussed, people taking prescribed doses of Valium or similar drugs can become physically, as well as psychologically, addicted.
- **Death:** Valium causes over 800 deaths a year. Over 300 of these are accidental overdoses, generally caused by taking Valium along with other drugs or alcohol.[10]

Chapters 2 and 3 of this book describe the dangers of Valium and the other benzodiazepines in detail.

The Sales—and Selling—of Valium

In 1980, Americans filled over 33 million prescriptions for Valium. They went home with a total of 1.8 billion pills. On top of this, they filled 38 million prescriptions for other tranquilizers and sleep aids in the Valium family. The total in this one year was over 70 million prescriptions, or 3.6 billion pills.[11]

Hoffmann-LaRoche, Valium's manufacturer, estimates that 8 million people use Valium. This means that the average Valium user takes 225 pills a year.

The annual cost of these drugs is staggering. Americans spent $293 million in 1980 on Valium alone—$800 thousand a day. Looking at the entire Valium family, Americans left their drugstores in 1980 with over $600 million worth of chemical calm.[12]

The high levels of stress and tension that Americans face have certainly helped the sales of anxiety-reducing drugs. But much of the success of these drugs, and especially the phenomenal success of Valium, is also the product of years of intense and skillful promotion.

From the early 1960s on, barrages of advertisements have given doctors the message, again and again, that pills—Valium or one of its family, of course—are the appropriate response to all kinds of personal difficulties or social stresses. Whether the problem was a frustrated housewife, a college student "apprehensive about unstable national and world conditions,"[13] or a "demanding and complaining patient"[14] who annoyed the doctor, the solution was a prescription for Valium or one of its chemical cousins.

Another set of advertisements has encouraged doctors to use drugs such as Valium for older people who "face not only the constraints brought about by their own reduced capabilities, but also those imposed by their social structure and environment."[15] Valium, like all benzodiazepines, is particularly dangerous in older people, and older people are significantly more likely to experience side effects, including confusion and drowsiness, when they take such drugs. These advertisements, however, call on doctors to extend their Valium prescribing even further into the lucrative "market" of older Americans—in spite of the considerable risks that benzodiazepines pose to the people who make up that market.

Doctors, notwithstanding the risks, have enthusiastically prescribed drugs like Valium for older people. The Food and Drug Administration revealed in 1978 that 44% of users of Valium and its cousins were 60 or older.[16]

Aggressive marketing—including not only advertisements but also gifts to doctors, "medical education" of doctors by drug companies, and detailmen, the door-to-door salesmen of drug companies—has paid off handsomely for Valium's manufacturer. From 1972 on, Valium has been the top-selling prescription drug in America.

Valium: Coping Through Chemicals

> *As things now stand, the tranquillizers may prevent some people from giving enough trouble, not only to their rulers, but even to themselves. Too much tension is a disease; but so is too little. There are certain occasions when we* ought *to be tense, when an excess of tranquillity (and especially of tranquillity imposed from the outside, by a chemical) is entirely inappropriate.*[17]
>
> —Aldous Huxley, *Brave New World Revisited*

Tension is a symptom. Feeling anxious is a sign that something is wrong, either within you or in your situation. Prescribing Valium or any tranquilizer for a situational problem is like giving a man with a broken leg morphine for his pain and telling him to keep walking.

In an article on the Valium family, Dr. Kenneth Solomon warns doctors of this pitfall. These drugs, he points out, "can be useful clinical tools. However, they should not be used as substitutes for effective psychotherapy, social solutions to social problems, solving one's problems of daily living, or appropriate evaluation of the uncooperative or annoying patient."[18]

The damage caused by using a pill to treat everyday stress—chemical coping—is not necessarily confined to the individual taking the drug. Dr. Donald Louria warns that using drugs to cope may also give an unintended message to your children:

> . . . if the mother is a daily tranquilizer user, then the child is three and a half times as likely to use opiates (such as heroin), five times as likely to use stimulants or LSD, seven times as likely to use tranquilizers as an appropriate control group whose mothers were not daily tranquilizer users.[19]

Chapter 4 of this book discusses what to do if you are anxious and thinking about using Valium or any tranquilizer.

The Rise and Fall of Valium and Its Chemical Cousins

With all the bad news, this book also gives some good news. Table II shows what has happened to prescriptions for Valium and its cousins over the past 17 years.

Since 1975, prescriptions for Valium and other benzodiazepines in this country have rapidly and consistently fallen. Total prescriptions for Valium fell 45%, from a high of 61 million in 1975 to 34 million in 1980.[20]

Table II

TOTAL PRESCRIPTIONS FOR VALIUM
AND ALL BENZODIAZEPINES
1964–1980

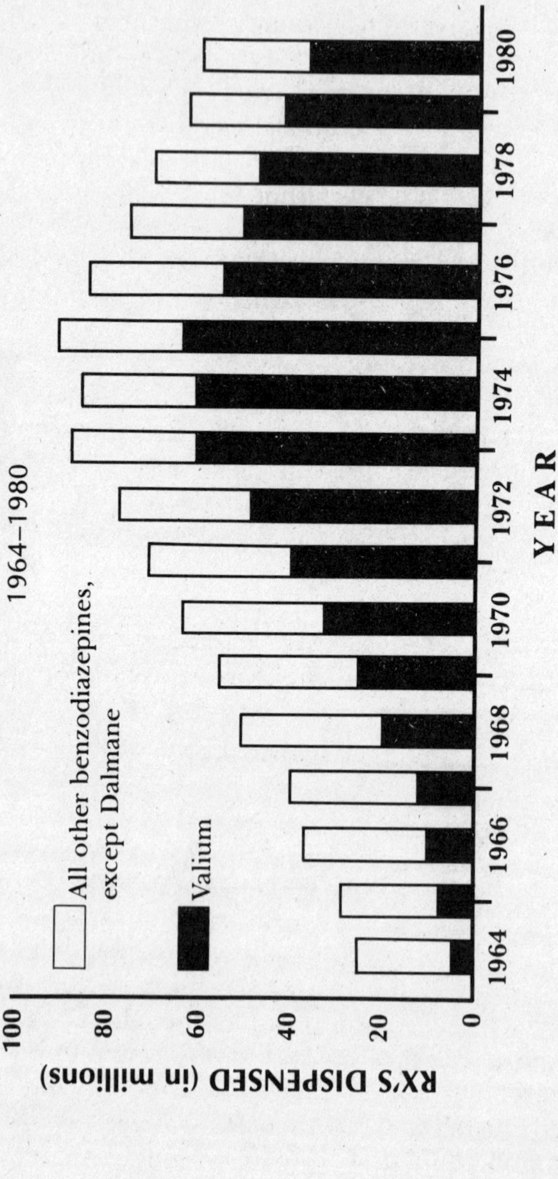

Source: National Prescription Audit, IMS America

The simple reason for this heartening change is a more informed public. As people have been informed about the dangers of Valium and similar drugs, many of them have decided that they can live—and even be happy—without this chemical crutch.

Valium and its chemical cousins certainly have some uses. But for many years, they have had far too many uses. As they learn the facts about Valium and the other benzodiazepines, people are better able to decide whether they really want to take these drugs. A great many of them have decided that they would rather not.

2

Is Valium Addicting?

I began taking [Valium] in 1970. My mother was critically ill. I could not handle the situation and I asked for a tranquilizer. They told me it was a non-addicting one. I tried to come off it myself, but could not.[1]

—A former Valium user

I took 5 milligrams of Valium four times a day for the first year, and then my dosage was increased to 10 milligrams four times a day for another 2 years. I decided that I was not nervous any more, so I did not need to take the pills, and I stopped. Five days later, I passed out, went into convulsions at work, and was admitted to a hospital for about 5 days . . . [My doctor] still says that they are not addictive.[2]

—Another former Valium user

The myth that Valium and other benzodiazepines are not addicting has been slow to die in medical circles. In spite of over 20 years of published reports showing addiction to benzodiazepines, some doctors continue to believe that these drugs are not—or hardly ever are—addictive.

The evidence shows just the opposite. Medical studies have shown that:

- Every drug in the Valium family can cause physical addiction. People who have stopped taking these drugs suddenly, after taking them for months, have developed serious withdrawal symptoms, including hallucinations and seizures.
- Low doses of Valium and its chemical cousins can cause both physical and psychological addiction. People who take prescribed doses for several months can become physically addicted.
- Anyone can get addicted to Valium and other benzodiazepines. Even if you have no mental or emotional problems, you can still become addicted.
- Thousands of people are—or have been—addicted to Valium and like drugs. And over 1 million Americans have taken these drugs long enough that they are in danger of becoming addicted.

Valium and the other benzodiazepines are not harmless cure-alls. Like other sedatives such as barbiturates and alcohol, these drugs are addictive. Considering their availability, that addiction is a serious public health problem.

Types of Drug Addiction

Drug addiction can take many forms. It can harm your mind, your body, or both. All of these problems can be related to drug addiction—separately or together—and can be caused by Valium or any benzodiazepine:

Habituation: needing a drug to feel better.

Tolerance: needing more and more of a drug to have the same effect.

Psychological addiction: craving a drug to the point where getting it may seem to be one of the most important things in your life.

Physical addiction or dependence: physically needing a drug, to the point where you develop distinctive physical symptoms if you stop taking it.

Withdrawal: the symptoms developed by a person who is addicted to a drug after stopping the drug. These symptoms are similar for all depressant or "downer" drugs, including barbiturates, alcohol, and Valium, and can include convulsions (seizures) and hallucinations.

The World Health Organization defines drug addiction or dependence as a

> state, psychic and sometimes physical—resulting from the interaction between a living organism and a drug, characterized by behavioral and other responses that always include a compulsion to take the drug on a continuous or periodic basis in order to experience its psychic effects and sometimes to avoid the discomfort of its absence.[3]

Addiction to Valium and Its Chemical Cousins: The Evidence

Since 1961, medical articles have described hundreds of people who were addicted to Valium. They have described both serious psychological addiction and potentially life-threatening physical addiction.

Danger at Low Doses

More alarming still are studies proving that low doses of drugs like Valium can also be addicting. Even if you never take more than your prescription calls for, you can still become addicted.

Addiction to low doses of Valium and other benzodiazepines may even be the major form of addiction to these drugs today. Of 80 cases of addiction to Valium reported to the Food and Drug Administration, 82% were taking doses in the usually prescribed range.[4]

As long ago as 1969, Dr. Jerome Levine, of the National Institute of Mental Health, warned that addiction to low doses of drugs like Valium was a known problem. He told a Senate subcommittee that, "it is now clear that with prolonged usage and/or high dosage, physiological dependence of the type known to occur with barbiturates is produced."[5]

In one study, 32 people who had taken an average of 10 mg of Valium daily for between 4 months and several years came to a clinic and suddenly stopped taking it. Almost half of these patients developed withdrawal symptoms, which included trouble sleeping, depression, headache, muscle twitching and pain, and seizures. The manufacturer recommends daily doses of Valium that may be as high as 40 mg per day.[6]

In another study, 23 of 24 people who sought help from a drug-treatment clinic, and who had taken an average of 16 mg of Valium daily for 1–96 months, developed withdrawal symptoms. They reported anxiety, restlessness, trouble sleeping, sweating, and other symptoms.[7]

A recent article describes 10 people who stopped Valium after using it for over a year. Their average daily Valium dose was 17 mg. All these patients had withdrawal symptoms, ranging from anxiety and restlessness to paranoia and loss of touch with reality. The article's authors warn that "more importantly, the changes on withdrawal of normal doses have in most cases been indistinguishable from those on withdrawal of high doses in other patients, either in quality or quantity."[8]

The message from these and countless other studies is clear. Valium and its chemical cousins are addictive, and you can become addicted even if you follow your doctor's instructions. *The Medical Letter* recently summed all this up: "All benzodiazepines can cause withdrawal reactions, including psychosis [insanity] and convulsions [seizures] . . . Reports such as these have led some *Medical Letter* consultants to recommend stopping these drugs as early as possible, with tapering after prolonged use."[9]

Danger with Continuing Use

Many of the people who have become addicted to Valium and other benzodiazepines have been taking them for a long time—often for several years. But addiction may develop over a few months, even at low doses.

One group of patients at a psychiatric center took 45 mg per day of Librium for 20 weeks and developed withdrawal symptoms when they stopped taking it.[10] (The label for Librium recommends daily doses as high as 100 mg.)

Low doses of Valium may be addictive just as quickly. People taking as little as 15 mg per day for a few months may develop typical withdrawal symptoms when they quit.

Sometimes it may take even less time. One young man who took 30 mg of Valium daily for three months had two seizures when he stopped taking Valium.[11]

The great majority of people who become addicted, though, have taken drugs like Valium for many months or years. Taking these drugs for more than a few weeks increases the risk of addiction. And since studies have not proven Valium and similar drugs to be effective for long-term use, it makes no sense at all to keep taking them in the face of their proven addictive risk.

Withdrawal Symptoms

I stopped, and for the first couple of weeks it was terror; multiple muscle contractions. I think one of the best descriptions I have heard is if somebody pours kerosene over your skin and then every so often they touch a torch to it or set it to fire; this is one of the feelings I had.

I became very paranoid; everybody was out to get me and nobody was a friend any longer. These kinds of things began to happen, and I became so uptight that I could not sleep; I could not eat. In the darkness of the night, I do not know whether I was actually hallucinating or I was having delusions, but they were a very frightening experience.[12]

—A former Valium user

If you have taken Valium or a similar drug for weeks or months and stop taking it, you can have severe withdrawal symptoms. These symptoms are serious—more serious than heroin-withdrawal symptoms.[13]

Withdrawal symptoms may start several days after you stop taking one of these drugs. Some of the members of the Valium family of drugs (Ativan, Serax, and Halcion) disappear from the body more rapidly and may produce withdrawal symptoms within a day.[14]

These withdrawal symptoms almost always include anxiety, restlessness, and trouble sleeping.[15] Headache, muscle twitching and pain, shaking, and changes in vision are also common.[16]

Many people going through benzodiazepine withdrawal experience various changes in sensation, including unpleasant feelings, tastes, or smells. They may become nauseated and vomit; they may also lose their appetite and lose weight. They often feel listless, depressed, and miserable.[17]

More dangerous reactions also occur. Benzodiazepine withdrawal can cause full-blown seizures.[18] It also can cause temporary insanity, including paranoia, hallucinations, and loss of touch with reality.[19]

If a person having withdrawal symptoms starts taking the drug again, the symptoms rapidly disappear. (This is a typical feature of withdrawal reactions.) Otherwise, without resuming drug use, the symptoms begin to get better after a week to ten days. They may take weeks or longer to disappear entirely.

How Many People Are Addicted?

Addiction has been infrequently reported at any dosage level. When seen, it has only been observed in patients who have used the drug over an extended period of time and at excessive doses.[20]

—Testimony of Robert B. Clark, President of Hoffmann-LaRoche [the manufacturer of Valium] before the U.S. Senate Subcommittee on Health and Scientific Research, September 10, 1979

You asked for a list of studies "which we did or may have supported" on dependence and long-term effects of Valium.

As far as I have been able to find out, Roche did not actively conduct or support such studies.[21]

—Interoffice memo, Hoffmann-LaRoche, August 24, 1979

The drug companies claim that hardly anyone gets addicted to drugs like Valium. Of course, it helps when they don't try too hard to find out about it.

What proof do they offer for their claim? One former employee of Hoffmann-LaRoche (the manufacturer of Valium) has written that fewer than 500 cases of Valium addiction have been reported to medical journals and government agencies. This, he says, shows that the risk from Valium is very low.[22]

Unfortunately, the vast majority of doctors do not report drug problems to the government and do not write journal articles. The reported cases, therefore, don't even scratch the surface of the problem of Valium addiction.

For example, a recent survey of 150 doctors in Texas found that 21 of them—14%—had treated at least one patient for tranquilizer withdrawal symptoms within the past year.[23] If this group is at all representative of the doctors in the rest of the country, 10 to 20 thousand or more people are being treated for benzodiazepine withdrawal in the U.S. each year in doctors' offices alone.

So how many people are addicted to Valium and other benzodiazepines? No one knows for sure, but we can get a few hints, in addition to what we learned from the Texas survey.

The DAWN Project

One hint comes from the Drug Abuse Warning Network, or DAWN. This U.S. government study collects information on drug abuse from selected hospital emergency rooms and medical examiners throughout the country.

In 1980 alone, these hospitals reported 16,605 emergency-room visits because of Valium abuse. *The entire family of drugs like Valium accounted for over 26,000 emergency-room visits.*[24]

In 17% of the 16,605 Valium-related visits, the patient had taken Valium because he or she was dependent on the drug. In other words, these emergency rooms saw people addicted to Valium *2,859 times* in 1980 alone.[25]

The hospitals that reported to DAWN only serve one-third of the country's population. This means that the real figures may be three times higher than this—*over 8,000 visits a year from people addicted to Valium.* Clearly, thousands of Americans must be addicted.

NIDA Statistics: Further Evidence of Addiction

Further evidence comes from the National Institute on Drug Abuse (NIDA), which collects information from federally funded drug-abuse treatment centers.

In 1979, these centers admitted 7,181 people for treatment of tranquilizer abuse. (Since the vast majority of tranquilizers prescribed today are members of the Valium family, most of these people were probably taking Valium or a similar drug.) Of these, 4,678 had never been treated before.[26]

1980 brought another 7,179 people to these treatment centers because of tranquilizer abuse. Of these, 4,573 were being treated for the first time.[27]

In these two years alone, then, such centers began treating over 9,000 Americans for tranquilizer abuse—people who had never been treated for this problem before.

FDA Figures: Hundreds of Thousands of People Are in Danger

People who take Valium or any benzodiazepine for several months, even at prescribed doses, can become addicted. People who exceed prescribed doses may become addicted even more quickly.

In 1979, the Food and Drug Administration looked at patterns of benzodiazepine use in the U.S. Their study revealed that

- 15% of people taking benzodiazepines in 1978 did so continuously for over four months. In other words, *1.5 million Americans* faced a serious risk of addiction to drugs like Valium.[28]

• 8% of benzodiazepine users—800,000 people—increased their dose over that prescribed by their doctor.[29]

These figures give an alarming view of benzodiazepine use in the U.S. In 1978 alone, over 1 million Americans who were taking these drugs were in danger of becoming addicted.

Thousands of Victims

No one knows exactly how many Americans are addicted to Valium and other benzodiazepines. The drug companies continue to claim that only a few "problem patients" develop addiction to Valium and its chemical cousins.

But these U.S. government statistics show just the opposite. Both DAWN and NIDA have found clear evidence that thousands of people are addicted to these dangerous drugs. Their addiction is severe enough that these people are going to emergency rooms and drug-treatment centers to get help. And FDA studies show that over 1 million people are in danger of becoming addicted.

Who Becomes Addicted?

True addiction is probably exceedingly unusual and, when it occurs, is probably confined to those individuals with "abuse-prone" personalities who ingest very large amounts.[30]

—Testimony of Robert B. Clark, President of Hoffmann-LaRoche [the manufacturer of Valium] before the U.S. Senate Subcommittee on Health and Scientific Research, September 10, 1979

One easy way to ignore a problem is to blame the victim. Doctors and drug companies have done this for years, pinning all the blame for benzodiazepine addiction on so-called "abuse-prone patients."

Their theory is simple: people who get addicted to Valium or one of its chemical cousins would become addicted to anything. No matter how inappropriately or excessively your doctor prescribes these drugs, if you are addicted, it's your own fault.

Their theory is also wrong. Medical studies have shown that people who have no history of drug problems can also become addicted to Valium, or to any benzodiazepine.

One recent study looked at 50 people who were taking Valium. It found that

- Half of these patients had increased their dose without asking their physician.
- Of 24 who tried to stop taking Valium, 22 (92%) were unable to do so. Twenty-three had withdrawal symptoms when they tried to stop.
- Only 7 of the 50 patients had any previous history of alcohol or drug problems. These were no more likely to have problems with Valium than were the others.[31]

The authors of this study concluded:

> It is disappointing to find no individual characteristics predictive of potential danger with diazepam (Valium) . . . In addition, many patients not thought to be "addiction-prone" developed what appeared to be both tolerance and withdrawal. These patients, given the drug for medical reasons and without a psychiatric history, were just as likely as psychiatric patients to develop tolerance and

> withdrawal. It appears as if the prescribing physician needs to cultivate as much care in prescribing diazepam as in other potential drugs of abuse.[32]

The few available statistics show that people who have trouble with Valium or other benzodiazepines are not distinguishable from other people who take these drugs. The majority are women; most are white. And—in sharp distinction to the statistics for other drugs of abuse—many people with Valium and other benzodiazepine drug problems are middle-aged or older. Of the women seen at NIDA treatment centers for tranquilizer abuse, 17 to 18% were 45 or older.[33]

Who becomes addicted to Valium and its chemical cousins? Anyone who takes these drugs in high doses, *or* anyone who takes them for a few months or more at any dose, can become addicted. The longer you take one of these drugs, the greater is your risk of addiction.

How Can I Tell if I Am Becoming Addicted?

You can be addicted and not know it. If you have taken Valium or any benzodiazepine for months, your body may become dependent on it. If you have taken one of these drugs daily for four months or more, addiction is a serious possibility.

Some of the warning signs of addiction are

· **Relying on the drug:** If you feel you need a drug like Valium to function, you may be addicted. You may feel that you can't cope at all without your daily pill. Or you may just think that you're not at your best without it. Either way, this drug has become a crutch for you. This is a danger sign.

• **Needing more to have the same effect:** All addicting drugs lose their effectiveness if you take them every day. This makes it tempting to keep taking more so that it will work as well as it did before. You are in particular danger if you are taking higher doses of Valium, or of any benzodiazepine, than your doctor has prescribed.

• **Not being able to quit:** When you are physically dependent on Valium or another benzodiazepine, quitting suddenly can make you downright sick. You feel tense and can't sleep, and you may go on to develop a full-blown withdrawal reaction—shakiness, headache, nausea, vomiting, changes in sensation, and, at times, hallucinations or seizures. When you resume taking the drug, the symptoms usually go away within 24 hours.

Withdrawal symptoms are a very serious danger sign. If you are physically addicted to Valium or another benzodiazepine, you should be under a doctor's care to withdraw from the drug safely.

If you have any of these warning signs, you may be addicted. Even if you don't, you are at risk if you have taken Valium or a related drug for several months.

Either way, it's time to find help and get to work on *stopping Valium.*

3

Other Dangers of Valium and Its Chemical Cousins

Every pill that you take is a trade-off. It offers a benefit: some action that you hope will help. At the same time, it carries a risk: it can cause a new problem or problems, some of which are much worse than your reason for taking the pill in the first place.

Valium and the other benzodiazepines are no exception. Addiction is just one of the risks that you take when you use these drugs. After you pay for your prescription, you continue to "pay" for its calming effect when you experience unwelcome side effects.

If you take Valium or any benzodiazepine, you can *expect*

- **Drowsiness:** Most people who take Valium—or any benzodiazepine—feel drowsy.[1]
- **Mental impairment:** Valium and like drugs predictably worsen memory and learning.[2] They also impair concentration and attention.[3]
- **Loss of coordination:** This can be very dangerous if you drive.[4]

Taking Valium or any benzodiazepine also carries other risks. These drugs may cause

- **Death:** Hundreds of people die each year as a result of taking Valium-type drugs. Many of these people die of accidental overdose when they take such drugs along with alcohol or other drugs.[5]
- **Hostility and attacks of rage:** This is hardly what you would expect from a tranquilizer, but it has happened repeatedly.[6]
- **Extreme confusion:** Elderly people taking Valium or other benzodiazepines have been mistakenly labeled senile.[7]
- **Birth defects and other problems in newborn infants:** The risk of birth defects appears to be greatest if you take Valium—or any other drug—during the first six weeks of pregnancy—a time when you may have no idea that you are pregnant.[8]

To decide whether you want to take Valium or any benzodiazepine, you need to know the risks. What follows is a summary of the known risks of these drugs.

Deaths Caused by Valium and Its Cousins

Taking too much Valium, or too much of any benzodiazepine, can kill you. It is less dangerous than taking a similar amount of barbiturates or antidepressants. But it can be fatal—especially if you have also taken alcohol or another drug. In 1980, over 800 people died as a result of taking Valium.[9]

In 1980, DAWN medical examiners reported 340 deaths related to Valium. Of these, 287 were felt to be caused by Valium. Seventeen deaths involved Valium only; in the others, the victims had also taken alcohol or another drug or drugs. Valium was the fourth most common drug related to death; it was exceeded only by alcohol in combination, heroin/morphine, and methadone.[10]

A large number of deaths due to Valium and similar drugs are not suicide attempts, but accidents. In 1980, DAWN medical examiners reported that 113 people had died *accidentally* as a result of taking Valium.[11] In other words, 41% of the deaths caused by Valium were accidental.

1980 DEATHS DUE TO VALIUM AND OTHER BENZODIAZEPINES—DAWN DATA

Valium	**Deaths in DAWN Population**	**Estimated Deaths in U.S.**
Total Valium-related deaths	340	1,020
Deaths *caused* by Valium	287	861
Accidental deaths caused by Valium	113	339
Deaths involving Valium only	17	51
Valium and Related Drugs		
Total deaths—Valium and the benzodiazepine family	481	1,443
Deaths *caused* by Valium and the benzodiazepine family	413	1,239
Accidental deaths caused by Valium and the benzodiazepine family	138	414

And the actual number of deaths caused each year by Valium is much higher. Since DAWN collects information on only one-third of the U.S. population, there were actually over 1,000 Valium-related deaths in this country in 1980 alone. Over 800 people died as a direct result of taking Valium, and over 300 of those were accidental.

As these figures show, Valium and its cousins cause hundreds of deaths each year. Most of these deaths result from taking these drugs along with alcohol or other drugs; many deaths are accidental.

Some of these deaths can be prevented by warning people about the danger of taking Valium along with other drugs. Another very effective way to prevent many deaths is to decrease the prescription and use of Valium. From 1978 to 1980, total prescriptions for Valium in the U.S. dropped from 44.9 million to 33.7 million per year.[12] At the same time, Valium-related deaths reported to DAWN dropped from 400[13] to 340[14]. Making people more aware of the dangers of Valium and the other benzodiazepines should further lower this tragic yearly toll of deaths.

Overdose and Abuse: Another Valium "Side Effect"

Every year, millions of people fill millions of prescriptions for Valium and other benzodiazepines. When a dangerous drug is so readily available, people are bound to be harmed by it. And they are. Thousands of people overdose on these drugs each year, both deliberately and accidentally.

From 1977 to 1980, DAWN reported over 16,000 emergency-room visits each year because of Valium problems, such as accidental overdose, deliberate overdose, and addiction.[15] Valium has remained the number-one drug involved in emergency-room visits, second only to alcohol in combination in number of mentions.[16]

In 1980, Valium was a problem in 16,605 emergency room visits. The entire Valium family of drugs received 26,397 mentions. Heroin and morphine, the next most common drugs of abuse, trailed well behind, with 8,680 visits.[17]

There are encouraging changes, though. From 1977 to 1980, as the number of Valium prescriptions has dropped, the number of emergency-room visits for Valium problems has also dropped—from 21,679 in 1977[18] to 16,605 in 1980.

Emergency-room visits where Valium was the only drug mentioned dropped also. In 1977, 8,807 emergency-room visits resulted from Valium use only. In 1980, Valium was the only drug mentioned in 5,314 visits.

Decrease in Valium Emergency-Room Visits

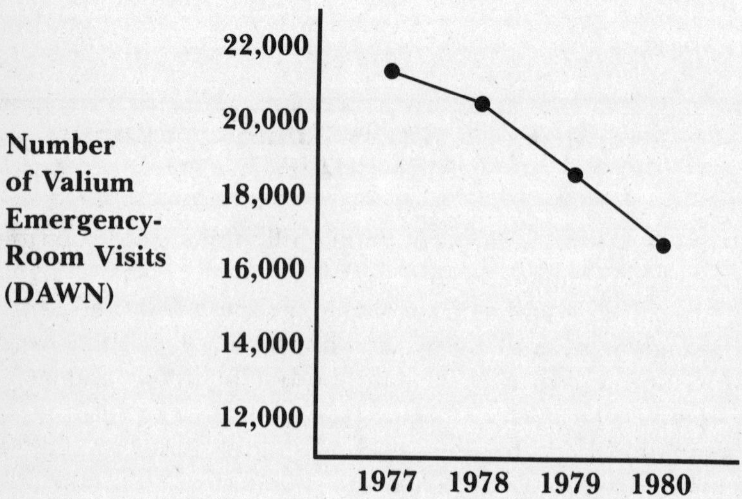

These drops in Valium abuse follow closely the drops in Valium prescriptions. Warning people about Valium's dangers and decreasing the number of prescriptions has clearly improved Valium's drug-abuse problem. But with over 16,000 Valium emergency-room mentions appearing each year, we still have a long way to go.

Decrease in Valium Prescriptions

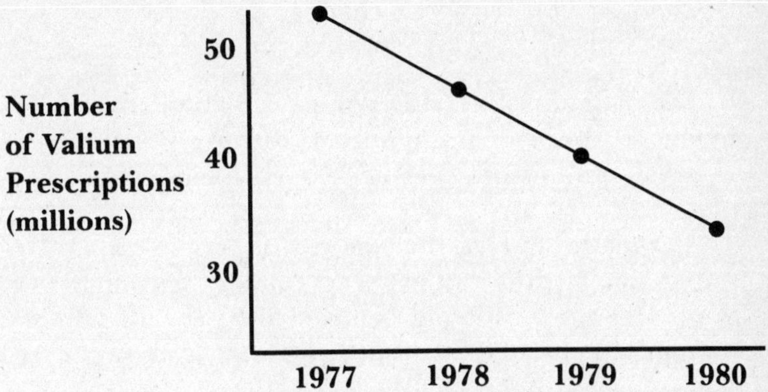

What Valium Does to Your Mind

> *I have also noticed over the period of one half year of being off them [Valium], that gradually month by month, my thinking has gotten clearer and clearer. And my bridge playing has improved two thousand percent and I am better at work. In every way, my thinking is better.*[19]
>
> —A former Valium user

The tranquilizing drugs, including Valium, have substantial effects on your mind. Many of these may be disturbing or downright dangerous.

Mental Problems Commonly Caused by Valium and Its Chemical Cousins

> *The patient was sleeping well, but had noticed loss of ability to concentrate. She no longer could read a book, although previously she had habitually read five or six weekly. Minor lapses of memory had been noted; she would start to look for something in the house and then forget what she was looking for.*[20]
>
> —Description of a Librium user (1963)

The patient just described was taking higher-than-recommended doses of tranquilizers. But even at the usual dose, Valium impairs alertness, coordination, learning, and memory.

As a matter of fact, the majority of people taking Valium or a similar drug can expect it to dull their minds. Dr. Nelson Hendler, testifying before a U.S. Senate subcommittee in 1979, stated:

> I would say that 75 or 80 percent of the patients taking Librium or Valium, or similar drugs, have impaired intellectual functioning and this occurs at normal, if you will, prescribing ranges—between 5 and 40 milligrams a day.[21]

Recent tests on animals have confirmed the serious effects that these drugs have on memory. In one test, rats took Valium at daily doses equivalent to a human dose of less than one 5 mg pill a day. After 2 weeks, their memories had significantly deteriorated. The authors of the study concluded: "This result indicates that a chronic treatment with diazepam causes functional modifications of the central nervous system resulting in a memory damage."[22]

These mental problems can be expected in many or most people while taking benzodiazepines such as Valium:

- **Drowsiness:** At least 1 in 5 people taking these drugs will be disturbed by drowsiness. In one study, the majority of users experienced this side effect.[23]
- **Fatigue:** Many people using drugs like Valium feel very weak and fatigued. Dizziness and lightheadedness are also common problems.[24]
- **Loss of coordination:** This is another common side effect. Many studies have found that people using drugs like Valium perform poorly on tests of psycho-motor coordination.[25]
- **Decreased ability to concentrate:** Both attention span and ability to concentrate may decrease in people who take benzodiazepines such as Valium.[26]
- **Impairment of memory and learning:** Usual doses of benzodiazepines such as Valium impair the ability to retain and to remember new information.[27] In each of 4 studies, memory was significantly worse in people who had taken Valium or one of its cousins.[28] Learning is also impaired after taking these drugs.[29]
- **Defects in speech:** Tests have shown that usual doses of drugs like Valium can make your speech less clear and harder to understand.[30]

Dangerous Mental Reactions to Valium and Its Chemical Cousins

Though less common, the other mental reactions to drugs like Valium may be severe or even life-threatening.

They include

• **Hostility and rage:** Although Valium and its cousins are supposed to be tranquilizers, some people feel more aggressive and hostile after taking these drugs. Some people react explosively to drugs like Valium; they become extremely excited, enraged, and even violent.

• **Confusion:** Some people—especially older people—become extremely confused when they take drugs like Valium.[31] Older people who are branded senile or depressed may turn out instead to be victims of benzodiazepine-induced confusion.

• **Suicide:** Some people taking drugs like Valium may become very depressed. A few of these people have committed suicide; the drug may have caused or intensified their suicidal thoughts.[32]

• **Nightmares:** Both sleep disturbances and nightmares may be side effects of drugs like Valium.[33]

Undesirable mental effects trouble a large number of Valium users. All are disturbing, and a few may be life-threatening. Whatever calming effects Valium offers should be weighed against the extremely frequent mental problems it causes. Dr. Nelson Hendler describes this trade-off:

> If, in fact, a man in business is complaining because he is having difficulties concentrating at work and he is feeling anxious, and then you prescribe Valium and you prescribe Valium for a long period of time—that is, 6 months or a year—you may, in fact, create the very condition that you are seeking to treat; that is, you may alter his concentration, you may impair his memory, and you may, in fact, help him to function less well rather than better.[34]

Driving and Valium: The Risks

In an actual driving test, people took Valium's sister drug Librium and then drove a car at low speeds. Their driving performance deterioriated visibly—and they did not realize it.[35]

More recently, a study found impaired driving ability in people who had taken Ativan, another benzodiazepine, in usual doses (3 mg a day) for 3 days. Both handling and braking ability were significantly impaired.[36]

Another study looked at tranquilizer use among people involved in traffic accidents. The risk of having a traffic accident was increased almost 5 times in people who had used a tranquilizer (usually one of the Valium family) in the past 3 months.[37]

Benzodiazepines such as Valium decrease attention and concentration,[38] slow reaction time,[39] and impair eye/hand coordination.[40] It is not surprising, then, that taking these drugs results in poor driving performance, both in laboratory studies and in real-life situations.[41]

Adding alcohol to Valium or to any benzodiazepine results in even greater danger. The combined damage from taking both these drugs at once seriously impairs the physical and mental skills required to drive safely.[42,43]

Driving while using Valium or any benzodiazepine is extremely risky. Your driving skills are weakened and your chance of an accident is increased. Driving after taking Valium, or another benzodiazepine, and alcohol is downright suicidal—as well as dangerous to others on the road. *Do not drive* at all if you take any Valium-type drug and have had a drink.

Valium and Your Baby: Pregnancy and Nursing

If you are (or might be) pregnant, Valium and its chemical cousins are particularly dangerous. Taking such drugs during early pregnancy may increase your child's risk of having birth defects. Taking them near delivery can give you a weak baby, who may be unable to feed or may even stop breathing. And if you take drugs like Valium continuously during late pregnancy, your child may have severe drug-withdrawal symptoms a few days after birth.

- **Birth defects:** Several studies have found that taking drugs like Valium early in pregnancy (in the first trimester, especially for the first 6 weeks) may increase the danger of birth defects. Two studies[44,45] found increases in cleft lip and cleft palate; one found an increased risk of severe malformations, such as mental retardation.[46] On the other hand, another study did not link these drugs to birth defects.[47] Still, the evidence of birth defects is strong enough that the FDA has warned that using drugs such as Valium in pregnancy "should almost always be avoided."[48]
- **Floppy baby:** Using Valium or similar drugs late in pregnancy, near delivery, has other dangers. The newborn infant may be weak and floppy, may suck poorly and be unable to get enough milk,[49] and may even have serious breathing problems.[50]
- **Withdrawal symptoms:** Several doctors have reported withdrawal symptoms in newborn infants when the babies' mothers took tranquilizers such as Valium continuously during late pregnancy. Dr. Loretta Finnegan described these babies: "They arch their backs, they have a large difficulty with feeding, and are much more difficult to treat than the infants undergoing heroin withdrawal."[51]

- **Nursing mothers:** Valium and other benzodiazepines get into mothers' milk. A nursing infant whose mother is taking these drugs will get a hefty dose. This will make the baby groggy; over time, the baby may eat poorly and lose weight.[52]

During pregnancy and nursing, you should take no drugs unless they are absolutely essential. Valium and the other benzodiazepines are rarely, if ever, essential, and their hazards are considerable. Do not take these drugs during pregnancy or while nursing.

Special Hazards for Older People

Valium and the other benzodiazepines are especially dangerous for older people. Several age-related changes make this a particularly poor time to take these drugs.

Studies have shown that older people taking Valium and its cousins are significantly more likely to have side effects.[53] One such side effect, confusion,[54] may lead old people to be falsely branded as senile. Stopping the drug will cure their "senility."

The risk involved in taking these drugs is even greater when an older person is taking other drugs. Since older people are more likely to be taking several drugs, they are particularly prone to develop dangerous drug interactions.

Valium, like other benzodiazepines, also stays in the body for a much longer time in the elderly. As a result, the drugs can accumulate to hazardous levels.[55] If an older person "must" have such a drug, the dose should be half the usual one.

At a July 28, 1980, meeting of the U.S. government

task force on sleep, Dr. William Dement discussed the problem of sleep apnea and Dalmane, one of Valium's cousins. Sleep apnea, or episodes of not breathing while asleep, is quite common in older people. When Dr. Dement gave Dalmane to two elderly people with this disorder, their episodes became alarmingly worse; one patient did not breathe for five minutes. Because of this danger, Dr. Dement told the task force that if he had to give an opinion at that time, he would say that people over 65 should not take Dalmane.[56]

Given the hazards the Valium family of drugs holds for the elderly, that warning could apply to more than just Dalmane. Some doctors feel that people over 65 should not take Valium or its cousins at all.

Other Dangers

The following problems have been linked to Valium, the most widely used benzodiazepine. Many of these problems have been linked with other benzodiazepines as well. These problems are not common, but they may be serious.

- **Jaundice and liver problems:** Valium may cause liver abnormalities and jaundice. People taking Valium for more than a few weeks should have periodic tests of liver function.[57]
- **Low blood counts:** Some people develop a low blood count while taking Valium. Since this can lower one's resistance to infection, people taking Valium for more than a few weeks should have a periodic blood count.[58]

• **Breathing problems:** People with severe lung disease, especially chronic bronchitis, should not use Valium. Valium decreases the urge to breathe; in the presence of lung disease, this can be life-threatening.[59]

• **Allergy and rash:** Valium may cause severe rash, hives, sudden shortness of breath, or other allergic reactions.[60]

• **Glaucoma:** Valium may cause an attack of glaucoma in people who have narrow-angle glaucoma.[61] People with this condition should not use Valium.[62]

• **Breast enlargement:** Several men have developed breast enlargement while taking Valium. When they stopped taking Valium, the enlargement gradually decreased or disappeared.[63]

• **Abnormal facial movements:** Doctors have described uncontrolled abnormal facial movements caused by Valium-type drugs.[64]

• **Cancer:** Oxazepam (Serax) caused liver tumors in one study in mice.[65] Since your body converts Valium, Librium, Tranxene, and Centrax into the same chemical as the drug called oxazepam, all of these drugs may carry the risk of causing cancer.

Interactions: Valium, Alcohol, and Other Drugs

• **Alcohol:** Valium and alcohol are a deadly combination.[66] Taking both of these "downers" at once can make you very drowsy; too much of this mixture can kill you. Since these two drugs together are particularly apt to slow your reaction time and impair your coordination, you should never drive or operate dangerous machinery if you have taken Valium—or any benzodiazepine—and alcohol.

• **Other sedatives:** Any sedative or "downer" can add to Valium's sedative effect.[67] At best, this mixture can cause drowsiness, loss of coordination, and slurred speech. At worst, mixing sedative drugs can cause accidental overdose and death. While taking Valium or any benzodiazepine, *do not take* (or ask your doctor before taking)

antidepressants	psychiatric drugs
antihistamines	seizure (epilepsy) medications
barbiturates	sleeping pills
narcotics	tranquilizers

• **Tagamet:** This ulcer drug keeps most members of the Valium family from leaving the body.[68] Because of this, a larger amount of the drug builds up; drowsiness and other problems will result. Ativan and Serax do not appear to have this effect.

• **Antabuse:** Like Tagamet, Antabuse keeps Valium-type drugs from leaving the body, so they can build up to dangerous levels. Again, this interaction probably does not occur with Ativan or Serax.[69]

• **Larodopa, Levodopa, Sinemet:** Valium may make these drugs (which treat Parkinson's disease) less effective.[70]

• **Birth control pills:** A recent study found that in women taking birth control pills, Valium stays in the body significantly longer. It may build up to dangerous levels.[71]

What You Aren't Being Told About Valium and Its Chemical Cousins

Knowing more about the medications you take is good for your health. Unfortunately, the drug companies think giving you this information isn't good for *their* health. So far, the drug companies have won—and the people who take Valium and its chemical cousins have lost.

On September 12, 1980, the Food and Drug Administration announced that it would require all new prescriptions for all benzodiazepines, such as Valium, and for several other drugs as well, to come with a Patient Package Insert (PPI).[72]

The PPI is a leaflet that you would get when filling a prescription for Valium or any benzodiazepine. It describes what the drug is, how to use it, who should avoid taking it, and what its dangers are.

Once the FDA rule went into effect, every new prescription for every benzodiazepine, including Valium, should have come with a PPI.

But under the Reagan administration, things suddenly changed. Drug companies, trade groups, and the American Medical Association pressured the FDA to suspend the rule and not require PPIs.

The pressure was effective. On December 22, 1981, after illegally suspending the regulation for nearly a year, the FDA announced that it was killing the rule. Now none of the drugs that the rule covered, including Valium and its cousins, will come with information for patients.

The decision to cancel these package inserts was a triumph for the drug industry—and a triumph for the old tradition of keeping patients uninformed. Thanks to this decision, the 5 million people who fill prescriptions for drugs such as Valium each month will *not* be able to read that

- "You can become dependent on Valium. Dependence is a craving for the drug or the inability to function normally without it."

• "An overdose of Valium alone or in combination with other drugs or alcohol can be fatal."

• "You should avoid drinking alcohol while taking Valium. The combination of alcohol and tranquilizers dangerously increases the effects of both."

• "Studies suggest an increased rate of birth defects in children whose mothers took Valium during the first three months of pregnancy."

• "If you have been taking Valium for a month or more, your doctor should reassess your condition and your continued use of the drug. The effect of these drugs for the relief of anxiety for periods longer than 4 months has not been studied."[73]

These are just a few of the facts that you would have learned from the canceled benzodiazepine Patient Package Insert—facts that the drug companies have fought vigorously to keep from you. Under the current administration, the companies have managed to keep patients from getting the PPI.

Fortunately, they have not succeeded entirely. Ever since 1975, prescriptions for Valium have been steadily dropping. More and more people have heard about the dangers of Valium—and have decided to quit.

4

Should I Ever Start Using Valium or Any of Its Chemical Cousins?

Everyone likes to feel good. Few people "enjoy" life crises or persistently high levels of anxiety. But life crises and anxiety, whether related to your job, your family, your friends, illness, or your attitude about yourself, are a fact of living for everyone. So what do we do about it? Learning to cope with the variety of external and internal problems that give rise to the uncomfortable feelings of stress or anxiety is one of the most difficult lessons we have to learn. "Working it out," "talking it through," "learning to live with it," changing jobs, friends, or living partners, recovering from or adjusting to an illness that is the main cause of your stress, or getting professional counseling from a medical doctor, a psychotherapist, or a member of the clergy are the more traditional ways that people have dealt with life crises and other anxiety-producing conditions.

Drugs, legitimate or otherwise, have always been used either to seek pleasure or to avoid tension and anxiety. In the last 25 years, though, there has been a striking new dimension added to the tension-tranquility equation. 1958 was the start of the most explosive growth of chemically induced tranquility ever seen. In a relatively short period, from 1958 to 1975, there was a fivefold increase in the use of minor tranquilizers in the United States, as measured by new prescriptions filled in retail drugstores in this country. This growth was headed by the tranquil trio of Miltown, Librium, and Valium. From 6 million *new* prescriptions filled in 1958, the number rocketed to 40 million by 1975.[1] During the same interval, there was also an increase in the consumption of alcohol, but it was only a small fraction of the growth of minor tranquilizer consumption.[2]

But just as rapidly as it rose during the interval between 1958 and 1975, minor tranquilizer consumption has fallen during the last 5 years, as discussed in the introduction. As mentioned previously, Valium itself fell 45%, from 61 million prescriptions filled (new and refills) in 1975 to 34 million in 1980.[3]

Deciding on Valium: Risks Versus Benefits

It is not surprising, given the increasing amount of evidence about the dangers of drugs like Valium, that fewer people are using them. But what if you are anxious or having difficulty coping and are not elderly, pregnant, or using alcohol or other drugs that should not be taken with Valium? Isn't Valium or one of its chemical cousins worth considering?

First, consider other solutions. Do you have somebody to talk to—a friend, a spouse, a family member, a professional counselor? Have you tried some form of regular exercise? Have you thought about getting a new job, if that is possible? Sometimes, when people think that there is a relatively "easy" answer—taking a pill—rather than more difficult solutions, which involve coping with causes rather than symptoms, they tend not to put as much energy into solving their problems.

If you read chapters 2 and 3, you are now aware of the risks involved in using benzodiazepine drugs such as Valium, and you also know that the best way of avoiding the risk of addiction, if you choose to use such a drug, is not to use it for too long a time. But what about the benefits or effectiveness of Valium? On a very short-term basis, there is no question that they may help some users to relieve anxiety and can also help people through an occasional sleepless night. However, there is no evidence that these drugs continue to have their tranquilizing effects for more than several months, or their sedative effects for more than a week or two—and there is a significant risk of addiction.

One very recent study looked at the effectiveness of Valium, two other tranquilizers, and a placebo (sugar pill) in treating anxiety in people going to the offices of a surgeon, an internist, or an obstetrician/gynecologist. At the end of the month, with weekly evaluations of the patients' anxiety levels being made by the patients themselves and by professional evaluators, the results showed "all four *treatments* to be efficacious in their therapeutic effects on relieving anxiety in non-psychiatric outpatients" (emphasis added).[4] In other words, people taking an average daily dose of Valium or similar tranquilizers improved no more rapidly than those who thought they were getting a tranquilizer but were really getting a sugar pill.

This study showed that the most important element of anxiety reduction was not the taking of a chemical such as Valium, but the process of talking with someone about anxiety and participating in an "experiment" in which the patient and others were involved in measuring relief.

But What if I Still Want to Take a Drug Like Valium?

If, at this point, you have guessed that we do not think people should use drugs such as Valium, you are right. But we know many doctors who practice what we consider good medicine, and who do prescribe Valium or one of its chemical cousins on occasion. Assuming that you know, from reading Chapter 3, which prescription drugs can have harmful interactions with drugs like Valium, and that people who use alcohol, older people, and pregnant and nursing women should not use these drugs, what further cautions will reduce the likelihood that you will be injured by these drugs? The following precautions, if your doctor does not already take them, can be strongly suggested by you, in your role of helping your doctor to practice better medicine.

Nine Rules for Safer Benzodiazepine Use

1. Ask your doctor not to write a prescription for more than 20 pills of Valium or other benzodiazepines for daytime use. This is enough for about 7 days. If the prescription is for a sleeping pill such as Dalmane, which is to be used only 1 pill at a time, the prescription should not be for more than 7 days' worth, or 7 pills. (The average prescription for Valium in 1980 was for 55 pills.)

2. Ask your doctor to write *No Refill* on the prescription, so that you will not be inclined, in case you become enamored of the good chemical feelings caused by the pills, to refill the prescription 5 times without seeing the doctor. (This dangerously lax refill policy is perfectly legal, because these drugs are not very carefully controlled by the government.)

By urging your doctor to write *No Refill,* you are telling him or her that you are more interested in a reevaluation, by you and the doctor, of how you are doing with your anxiety, than in an unevaluated continuation of use of the drug, which could be the first step toward addiction or other problems.

3. At the end of the first day and every day you are using Valium or any benzodiazepine, evaluate what you have done, on your own or by talking to others, to find out what is making you anxious, and evaluate what you have done to alter the internal or external circumstances that are causing your anxiety. Keep a record of these evaluations.

4. As soon and as often as possible, try to reduce the dose you are taking, in consultation with your doctor. Since you only have enough for one week, it is most unlikely that you will have become addicted to Valium in this short interval.

Although the following rules for safer benzodiazepine use are discussed in greater detail in Chapter 3, they are repeated here in summary form for Valium. They all apply to the other benzodiazepines as well.

5. If you use Valium, do not drive a car or operate dangerous machinery.[5]

6. If you use Valium, do not drink alcohol.[6]

7. If you are elderly, pregnant or nursing, or have narrow-angle glaucoma or serious lung disease, you should not use Valium.[7]

8. Unless you have consulted your doctor, while taking Valium, do not take drugs that have a sedative or "downer" effect.[8] These include

- antidepressants
- antihistamines
- barbiturates
- narcotics
- psychiatric drugs
- seizure (epilepsy) medications
- sleeping pills
- tranquilizers

9. The following drugs should also not be used with Valium:

Tagamet, Antabuse, birth control pills. These drugs keep one or more drugs of the benzodiazepine family from leaving your body. Because of this, the drugs build up in the body; drowsiness or other side effects may result.[9,10,11]

Larodopa, Levodopa, Sinemet. Valium may make these drugs (which treat Parkinson's disease) less effective.[12]

The following is an exact replication of the *physician labeling* for Valium. Similar labeling exists for Ativan, Centrax, Dalmane, Halcion, Librium, Paxipam, Restoril, Serax, Tranxene, and Xanax.

VALIUM® TABLETS (diazepam/Roche) ⓒⅣ

Valium Tablets is a product of Roche Products Inc., Manati, P.R. 00701.

The following text is complete prescribing information based on official labeling in effect August 1, 1981.

Description: Valium (diazepam/Roche) is a benzodiazepine derivative developed through original Roche research. Chemically, diazepam is 7-chloro-1,3-dihydro-1-methyl-5-phenyl-2H-1,4-benzodiazepin-2-one. It is a colorless crystalline compound, insoluble in water and has a molecular weight of 284.74.

Pharmacology: In animals Valium appears to act on parts of the limbic system, the thalamus and hypothalamus, and induces calming effects. Valium, unlike chlorpromazine and reserpine, has no demonstrable peripheral autonomic blocking action, nor does it produce extrapyramidal side effects; however, animals treated with Valium do have a transient ataxia at higher doses. Valium was found to have transient cardiovascular depressor effects in dogs. Long-term experiments in rats revealed no disturbances of endocrine function.

Oral LD_{50} of diazepam is 720 mg/kg in mice and 1240 mg/kg in rats. Intraperitoneal administration of 400 mg/kg to a monkey resulted in death on the sixth day.

Reproduction Studies: A series of rat reproduction studies was performed with diazepam in oral doses of 1, 10, 80 and 100 mg/kg. At 100 mg/kg there was a decrease in the number of pregnancies and surviving offspring in these rats. Neonatal survival of rats at doses lower than 100 mg/kg was within normal limits. Several neonates in these rat reproduction studies showed skeletal or other defects. Further studies in rats at doses up to and including 80 mg/kg/day did not reveal teratological effects on the offspring.

In humans, measurable blood levels of Valium were obtained in maternal and cord blood, indicating placental transfer of the drugs.

Indications: Valium is indicated for the management of anxiety disorders or for the short-term relief of the symptoms of anxiety. Anxiety or tension associated with the stress of everyday life usually does not require treatment with an anxiolytic.

In acute alcohol withdrawal, Valium may be useful in the symptomatic relief of acute agitation, tremor, impending or acute delirium tremens and hallucinosis.

Valium is a useful adjunct for the relief of skeletal muscle spasm due to reflex spasm to local pathology (such as inflammation of the muscles or joints, or secondary to trauma); spasticity caused by upper motor neuron disorders (such as cerebral palsy and paraplegia); athetosis; and stiff-man syndrome.

Oral Valium may be used adjunctively in convulsive disorders, although it has not proved useful as the sole therapy.

The effectiveness of Valium in long-term use, that is, more than 4 months, has not been assessed by systematic clinical studies. The physician should periodically reassess the usefulness of the drug for the individual patient.

Contraindications: Valium is contraindicated in patients with a known hypersensitivity to this drug and, because of lack of sufficient clinical experience, in children under 6 months of age. It may be used in patients with open angle glaucoma who are receiving appropriate therapy, but is contraindicated in acute narrow angle glaucoma.

Warnings: Valium is not of value in the treatment of psychotic patients and should not be employed in lieu of appropriate treatment. As is true of most preparations containing CNS-acting drugs, patients receiving Valium should be cautioned against engaging in hazardous occupations requiring complete mental alertness such as operating machinery or driving a motor vehicle.

As with other agents which have anticonvulsant activity, when Valium is used as an adjunct in treating convulsive disorders, the possibility of an increase in the frequency and/or severity of grand mal seizures may require an increase in the dosage of standard anticonvulsant medication. Abrupt withdrawal of Valium in such cases may also be associated with a temporary increase in the frequency and/or severity of seizures.

Since Valium has a central nervous system depressant effect, patients should be advised against the simultaneous ingestion of alcohol and other CNS-depressant drugs during Valium therapy.

Physical and Psychological Dependence: Withdrawal symptoms (similar in character to those noted with barbiturates and alcohol) have occurred following abrupt discontinuance of diazepam (convulsions, tremor, abdominal and muscle cramps, vomiting and sweating). These were usually limited to those patients who had received excessive doses over an extended period of time. Although infrequently seen, milder withdrawal symptoms have also been reported following abrupt discontinuance of benzodiazepines taken continuously, generally at higher therapeutic levels, for at least several months. Consequently, after extended therapy, abrupt discontinuation should generally be avoided and a gradual tapering in dosage followed. Particularly addiction-prone individuals (such as drug addicts or alcoholics) should be under careful surveillance when receiving diazepam or other psychotropic agents because of the predisposition of such patients to habituation and dependence.

***Usage in Pregnancy:* An increased risk of congenital malformations associated with the use of minor tranquilizers (diazepam, meprobamate and chlordiazepoxide) during the first trimester of pregnancy has been suggested in several studies. Because use of these drugs is rarely a matter of urgency, their use during this period should almost always be avoided. The possibility that a woman of childbearing potential may be pregnant at the time of institution of therapy should be considered. Patients should be advised that if they become pregnant during therapy or intend to become pregnant they should communicate with their physicians about the desirability of discontinuing the drug.**

Management of Overdosage: Manifestations of Valium overdosage include somnolence, confusion, coma and diminished reflexes. Respiration, pulse and blood pressure should be monitored, as in all cases of drug overdosage, although, in general, these effects have been minimal following overdosage. General supportive measures should be employed, along with immediate gastric lavage. Intravenous fluids should be administered and an adequate airway maintained. Hypotension may be combated by the use of Levophed® (levarterenol) or Aramine (metaraminol). Dialysis is of limited value. As with the management of intentional overdosage with any drug, it should be borne in mind that multiple agents may have been ingested.

Precautions: If Valium is to be combined with other psychotropic agents or anticonvulsant drugs, careful consideration should be given to the pharmacology of the agents to be employed—particularly with known compounds which may potentiate the action of Valium, such as phenothiazines, narcotics, barbiturates, MAO inhibitors and other antidepressants. The usual precautions are indicated for severely depressed patients or those in whom there is any evidence of latent depression; particularly the recognition that suicidal tendencies may be present and protective measures may be necessary. The usual precautions in treating patients with impaired renal or hepatic function should be observed.

In elderly and debilitated patients, it is recommended that the dosage be limited to the smallest effective amount to preclude the development of ataxia or oversedation (2 mg to 2½ mg once or twice daily, initially, to be increased gradually as needed and tolerated).

The clearance of Valium and certain other benzodiazepines can be delayed in association with Tagamet (cimetidine) administration. The clinical significance of this is unclear.

Adverse Reactions: Side effects most commonly reported were drowsiness, fatigue and ataxia. Infrequently encountered were confusion, constipation, depression, diplopia, dysarthria, headache, hypotension, incontinence, jaundice, changes in libido, nausea, changes in salivation, skin rash, slurred speech, tremor, urinary retention, vertigo and blurred vision. Paradoxical reactions such as acute hyperexcited states, anxiety, hallucinations, increased muscle spasticity, insomnia, rage, sleep disturbances and stimulation have been reported; should these occur, use of the drug should be discontinued.

Because of isolated reports of neutropenia and jaundice, periodic blood counts and liver function tests are advisable during long-term therapy. Minor changes in EEG patterns, usually low-voltage fast activity, have been observed in patients during and after Valium therapy and are of no known significance.

Dosage and Administration: Dosage should be individualized for maximum beneficial effect. While the usual daily dosages given below will meet the needs of most patients, there will be some who may require higher doses. In such cases dosage should be increased cautiously to avoid adverse effects.

	USUAL DAILY DOSE
Adults: *Management of Anxiety Disorders and Relief of Symptoms of Anxiety.*	Depending upon severity of symptoms—2 mg to 10 mg, 2 to 4 times daily
Symptomatic Relief in Acute Alcohol Withdrawal.	10 mg, 3 or 4 times during the first 24 hours, reducing to 5 mg, 3 or 4 times daily as needed
Adjunctively for Relief of Skeletal Muscle Spasm.	2 mg to 10 mg, 3 or 4 times daily
Adjunctively in Convulsive Disorders.	2 mg to 10 mg, 2 to 4 times daily
Geriatric Patients, or in the presence of debilitating disease.	2 mg to 2½ mg, 1 or 2 times daily initially; increase gradually as needed and tolerated
Children: Because of varied responses to CNS-acting drugs, initiate therapy with lowest dose and increase as required. Not for use in children under 6 months.	1 mg to 2½ mg, 3 or 4 times daily initially; increase gradually as needed and tolerated

How Supplied: For oral administration Valium scored tablets—2 mg, white; 5 mg, yellow; 10 mg, blue—bottles of 100* and 500;* Prescription Paks of 50, available in trays of 10.* Tel-E-Dose® packages of 100, available in trays of 4 reverse-numbered boxes of 25,† and in boxes containing 10 strips of 10.†

We do not advocate banning Valium or any benzodiazepine. But we do think the benzodiazepines are used far too much. Informed patients can help their doctors to eliminate unnecessary use and make these minor tranquilizers even more minor—in terms of use—than they are now.

5

Stopping Valium

This chapter is for the tens of millions of you who are now using Valium or one of its chemical cousins and who want to stop, think you might want to stop, or think you want to keep taking these drugs but are afraid of what might happen if you stop for any reason. There is no question that the shorter the period of time that you have been using a benzodiazepine, the easier it will be to stop. As discussed in Chapter 4, if your doctor gives you a prescription that lasts only for a week, it is highly unlikely that in that short a period of time you will become physically addicted to the drug.

Even if you take just 1 pill a day for 3 weeks, instead of 3 a day for 1 week, it is still unlikely that you will have become addicted in that period of time. So if you just had the one prescription for 20 pills filled, and, at your insistence, the doctor wrote *No Refill* on the prescription, you are almost certainly not addicted and should find it relatively easy to stop using Valium or any other benzodiazepine. To repeat what we recommended in the 9 Rules for Safer Benzodiazepine Use:

At the end of each day you are using Valium, evaluate what you have done, on your own or by talking to others, to find out what is making you anxious, and evaluate what you have done to alter the internal or external circumstances that are causing your anxiety. Keep a record of these evaluations. As soon and as often as possible, try to reduce the dose you are taking, in consultation with your doctor.

Even though you will not become addicted in a week or two, what is the shortest period of time in which you can become addicted to Valium or another benzodiazepine? We pointed out earlier, in Chapter 2, that after 4 months of use, even at the recommended dose, there is a strong likelihood of becoming addicted.

Although 4 months is frequently referred to as the "magic time"—the implication being that if you use the drug for less than 4 months, it is not likely you will become addicted—there is reason to believe that it is entirely possible to develop addiction within a shorter period of time. A study done in 1969 showed withdrawal symptoms in patients using Librium for 2½ to 3 months.[1] Considering what is known about patterns of addiction to other substances, such as alcohol and barbiturates, it is very likely that if such a study were done today, we would find that after 1 or 2 months, a significant number of people using Valium or another benzodiazepine had become addicted.

So if you think you may be addicted (see in Chapter 2, How Can I Tell If I Am Becoming Addicted?) and would like to do something about it, you should first have a talk with your doctor. Depending on what kind of doctor you have, you will get a receptive or not-so-receptive response. What follows are scenarios, each representing a type of doctor or situation you may encounter.

Conversations with Three Doctors

Scenario A: Doctor Knows Best?

Edith has had a rocky year. Her divorce became final after years of bitter wrangling with her now ex-husband. Required to work for the first time in her life, she started out as a salesperson in a boutique. Thanks to her natural feeling for fashion, she was soon promoted to buyer and assistant manager.

The divorce, her job, her relationship with two lively children now entering adolescence, and her reentry into the "singles" scene have all been sources of anxiety as Edith has attempted to cope with the many changes in her life.

About two years ago, when it was clear that her marriage was breaking up, Edith went to see her doctor about a backache brought on by strenuous household work. During the conversation she told her doctor about the tension at home. Her doctor gave her a prescription for Valium to help with both problems. At first the prescription was for 5 mg 3 times a day, and it made Edith feel more in control of her life; but mounting tension at home, protracted legal proceedings, and ultimate entry into the job world all increased her anxiety, until her doctor suggested that more Valium might be in order. Now she is taking one 10 mg pill 4 times a day, which is what her doctor prescribed.

On a recent buying trip for the boutique, Edith picked up a book at the airport—an autobiography of a professional woman who had become addicted to Valium. She noticed the parallels between her life and the author's, and when she returned from the trip she made an appointment with her doctor.

Edith: Doctor, I'm worried about the Valium I'm taking. I've been taking Valium for over two years now, and I wonder if I could be getting addicted.

Doctor: Well, now, Edith, I guess you've been reading some of those scare stories in the popular press.

Edith: Yes, I have, Doctor. I read a book about a woman a lot like me who began taking Valium because of the stress in her life and wound up in terrible shape when she tried to quit. Ann Landers wrote a warning about Valium, too, and now I'm worried.

Doctor: Well, I can assure you, dear, that I keep right up to date with professional literature—not the headline-making stuff you've been reading—and there isn't really any danger.

Edith: But, Doctor, I asked the druggist about this, and he showed me a book called the *Physicians' Desk Reference*—see, just like the one over there on your shelf—and it said that I was taking the maximum dosage permitted, and that even the manufacturer doesn't know very much about the long-term effects of the drug. The book also said I shouldn't be taking it with alcohol. I had two glasses of wine with dinner just a few days ago.

Doctor: And did anything bad happen?

Edith: Well, no, not really, but—

Doctor: So you see, it's perfectly safe!

Edith: The book the druggist showed me also said I should be careful driving. I do a lot of driving as part of my job.

Doctor: And have you had an accident?

Edith: Well, no, but maybe I've been lucky.

Doctor: I don't see why you're complaining. These pills are doing you good, and I don't understand why you're taking up my time with silly questions.

Edith: No, I'm worried about taking these pills. I think it's bad for me to be taking them for such a long time. My life is on a pretty even keel now, and I don't think I need a crutch; in fact, I wonder if I ever really did. I know now I could have used a counselor during the time of my divorce, but no one ever suggested it, and I didn't know enough to think of it myself. I really don't like the idea of using chemicals like this, and I think it would be best if I stopped using Valium.

Doctor: Oh, you do, eh—now, where did you get *your* medical degree, little lady? Don't you think I know what's best for you?

Edith: Oh, Doctor, I don't want to have a fight over this, but I would like your help. I know I still have some personal problems, but my back feels fine now, and perhaps with counseling—

Doctor: I can see you are not interested in my advice. Well, then, do whatever you want to do. If you don't want to take the pills, just don't take them. I don't care. It's your problem; just don't come back here. I think the appointment is over.

Edith: But, Doctor—is it safe to just stop all of a sudden like that? Couldn't I get withdrawal symptoms?

Doctor: If you really wanted my advice, you would have taken it, and continued with your pills, just as I prescribed. I'm really very busy now; good day.

Edith left the doctor's office. She still had 1 refill of her Valium prescription, so she continued using it as directed. However, she went directly to a drug-information hotline for a referral to a physician who would help her get off Valium safely. She was lucky, for if she had followed her doctor's advice and quit cold turkey, she might have had severe withdrawal symptoms.

Scenario B: Working with the Doctor

Ann is a housewife and mother of three. Two years ago, her doctor prescribed Valium for her after one of her children was seriously injured in an accident. The child is now fine, but keeping a home and raising 3 children has brought many new stresses, and Ann is always expected to be friendly and responsible. Valium seems to help, so her doctor has kept giving her prescriptions for Valium and she has continued to take it. She takes Valium only as directed: a 10 mg pill 2 to 3 times a day.

Ann also has had several attacks of low back pain since she hurt her back a few years ago. Her doctor told her that Valium will help her back pain, too.

Recently Ann read articles warning that Valium can be addicting. Although she is taking it only as prescribed, she is worried. After some thought, Ann wrote down a list of questions and decided to talk to her doctor about Valium.

Ann: Doctor, I recently read that taking Valium can make people addicted. I've been taking the Valium you prescribed for me for two years now, and I'm a little worried. Could I be getting addicted to Valium?

Doctor: You certainly shouldn't take more Valium than you need, Ann, but Valium is actually quite safe. Very few people get addicted to Valium. And people who do get addicted are usually those who take very high doses of Valium.

Ann: I understand that. But I've read that even doses of Valium prescribed by doctors can be dangerous if I take them for a long time. Isn't two years getting to be a long time?

Doctor: Well, yes, it's a pretty long time. You certainly don't want to take it if you don't need it. But if you do need a drug for tension, it's really a pretty safe drug.

Ann: Is it really safe? I've read that Valium can affect my mind—that it could make my memory worse, or make it harder for me to think clearly. I do seem to forget things more than I did. Could that be the Valium?

Doctor: Well, many things can make you forgetful, and I wouldn't just blame the drug. Valium does seem to have some effects on a few people's mental functions. But so does anxiety! It's very hard to think well when you're upset.

Ann: That's true, but I do worry about muddling up my mind even more. And I'm also worried about drowsiness. I do feel a little slow sometimes after taking Valium. Is it safe for me to drive?

Doctor: It *is* pretty common for Valium to slow you down. Some studies even suggest that it slows your reactions and may affect your coordination. You certainly don't want to drive when you're at all drowsy—or to take anything else that could make you drowsy when you're taking Valium.

Ann: You mean things like sleeping pills?

Doctor: Yes, sleeping pills. And also alcohol, and other tranquilizers. And antihistamines, too.

Ann: What are antihistamines?

Doctor: They're drugs for allergies. But a lot of cold medicines have antihistamines in them, too. Taking those with Valium can make you even drowsier.

Ann: I'm glad you told me that. But it does worry me—I often have my children in the car with me, and I'd hate to drive if I'm not completely alert. I'm still a little worried about addiction, too. Wouldn't taking a tranquilizer for this long change my system somehow? Ten milligrams of Valium used to knock me out, and now I take it and hardly notice the difference.

Doctor: It's true, you do seem to get used to a drug when you take it for a long time.

Ann: Then is it really worth the risk? If it can slow me down, and if there's even a small chance I could get addicted, should I be taking a drug like this?

Doctor: That depends on whether you need it.

Ann: Does it even work when you take it for this long? It really knocked me out at first, but is it doing anything now?

Doctor: It's hard to say. The label does say that it hasn't been studied well for periods of over four months.

Ann: Do you have a copy of the label that I can see? My bottle just says: "Take 1 pill 2 or 3 times a day as needed."

Doctor: You can get the label from your pharmacist. But it's written for doctors, and you may find it hard to read.

Ann: Can I call you if I have any questions?

Doctor: Of course.

Ann: But back to Valium—if you're not sure it's doing

anything, and if it can be dangerous, wouldn't I be better off trying to do without it?

Doctor: Well, if you'd like to try, it might be a good idea to try to cut down.

Ann: How about trying to do without it entirely?

Doctor: You could try that, too, if you want.

Ann: Can I just quit cold turkey?

Doctor: Well, it might not be a good idea. If you stop taking Valium suddenly after two years, you may have bad reactions. You may get nervous or shaky or have trouble sleeping.

Ann: It sounds like I could be a little addicted, then.

Doctor: Well, you're used to the drug. And it could just be your old anxiety coming back.

Ann: But I wasn't that anxious before my son was hurt. And since then, I've been taking Valium all the time.

Doctor: You're used to taking Valium, too. So it's better if you cut back gradually.

Ann: How should I take it when I'm cutting back? I'm taking 2 to 3 pills a day.

Doctor: You want to lower your dose over about a 4-week period. So take 2 pills a day for a week; then take 1½ pills a day for the next week. Then take 1 pill a day or ½ a pill twice a day for a week. Then cut down to ½ a pill a day for a week, and then stop.

Ann: Will I have problems right away if I quit suddenly?

Doctor: No. If you stop taking Valium after taking it a long time, it stays in your body in some form for over a week. So it takes a few days before you develop symptoms.

Ann: But I've heard that you can still get withdrawal symptoms.

Doctor: Well, if you were addicted, you could get severe symptoms. They start a few days after you stop.

Ann: What about my back pain? Will that get worse if I don't use Valium?

Doctor: Valium is only one of the treatments for back pain, and it shouldn't be used alone. Aspirin, rest, and heating pads are very helpful, and they probably will be all you need. You should also be doing back exercises to keep your back from acting up. I can give you a sheet describing some back exercises, if you'd like.

Ann: That would be nice. What about tension? What can I do for tension besides take pills?

Doctor: It depends on what causes it. If you have serious problems, you may want to get counseling. If someone upsets you, try talking to that person. When you can do it, changing situations that upset you is the best thing to do to help tension.

Ann: That makes sense to me. I think I could really use a week's vacation. I haven't had a vacation in years!

Doctor: It sounds like a good idea.

Ann: It sounds much better to me than taking pills. I really like the idea of getting off this Valium. I've felt sort of guilty about it—as if it's a crutch. But I'd feel a lot more free if I could do without it. I do want to quit—even though it's a little scary.

Doctor: You seem to have thought about it a lot. And I'll be happy to try to help you through the rough spots if you find you have trouble quitting.

Ann: Good. I need your help.

Doctor: Let me write down a schedule for cutting down, and I'll see you in a month. Give me a call if you have any problems while you're cutting down your dose.

Ann: Thanks. I will.

Doctor: You may find that you need to cut down your dose more slowly. Don't feel that you need to keep to this schedule. Some people take months to stop entirely.

Ann: I'll see how I do.

Doctor: I'll see you in a month, but call me sooner if you have any problems.

Ann: See you then. Hey! I'm leaving here without any prescriptions at all! I feel better already.

Scenario C: The Tension of Business

George is an office-machine salesman in a large eastern city. His job demands minute attention to detail, full awareness of his customers' needs, and constant watchfulness to keep competitors from taking over his accounts. Most of his income consists of commissions on sales, and he is under constant pressure to add to his accounts to meet the needs of his growing family.

Recently, George learned that he has high blood pressure. His doctor suggested that he lose 25 pounds and limit the salt in his diet. George has lost about 15 pounds so far and has been very careful about his salt intake, even though his job makes it difficult for him to avoid eating quick snacks and processed foods.

About 6 months ago, George began experiencing severe stomach pains late at night and early in the morning. His doctor ordered gastrointestinal X rays, which revealed a duodenal ulcer. He was treated for 6 weeks with a drug called Tagamet; now he takes antacids as needed.

Four months ago, George's doctor suggested that he take a drug called Ativan, a chemical cousin to Valium. The doctor said that this drug would make George less anxious and thus help his high blood pressure and his ulcer.

George took the pills 3 times a day, as prescribed. They seemed to make him feel a bit more calm, and his wife thought he was less impatient with their children. But he also had the feeling that he was often not completely alert, or that he was running around in a fog. Since coffee was also forbidden because of his ulcer, this was no small problem. But his doctor reassured him that this drowsiness would decrease if he continued to take Ativan.

Now, 4 months after starting to take Ativan, George is at his doctor's office for a checkup.

Doctor: I'm happy to tell you that your blood pressure is very good today. How are you doing with your stomach pains?

George: Not too badly. I have pain at times, but it goes away when I take an antacid.

Doctor: Are you taking the Ativan as I prescribed?

George: That's what I need to talk to you about. You were right about the drowsiness—it seems to have decreased. But I still don't feel quite right.

Doctor: What do you mean?

George: I need to stay on top of things at work, and I don't think I'm doing that as well. A few days ago, one of my customers called me with an order, and I forgot some of the things he told me!

Doctor: That's a problem. But are you sure the Ativan is at fault? You need to keep up with a lot of things at work.

George: I don't know. But ever since I've been on Ativan, I feel slow. I can't concentrate as well. And I do seem to forget things more. Do I really need to be on this drug for my blood pressure? How much good is it really doing?

Doctor: Being anxious can make your blood pressure go up, and this medication can make you less anxious. Since you do have a high-stress job, I thought some of your high blood pressure might be due to stress.

George: But being overweight can raise my blood pressure, too. So can salt in my diet. You told me that.

Doctor: Yes, that's true.

George: I've done what you told me to do. And I can tell you, it's not easy to lose 25 pounds. But it's easier than working in a fog.

Doctor: This seems to be a real problem for you. But your high-stress life-style still concerns me. The medical proof may not be conclusive, but I feel that constant anxiety may have something to do with your ulcer, too.

George: Then Ativan is a treatment for my ulcer, too?

Doctor: To be honest, it's never been shown to help ulcers. But when I see a very tense person with ulcers, it makes sense to me to try to reduce that tension.

George: If I keep on forgetting things, I'll get a lot more tense.

Doctor: I can see that you don't want to take Ativan. I don't have solid proof that it's helping your ulcer or your high blood pressure, but I also know you work under an unhealthy amount of pressure. How about taking Ativan at a lower dose?

George: I'd rather just quit. I'll keep losing weight and stay on the low-salt diet. I can take antacids every day if you want. And you can check my blood pressure and see what happens.

Doctor: I guess it's worth a try. But we need to think about your work problem. Do you really need this breakneck pace to meet your monthly bills? Are the bill collectors beating on your door?

George: Well, to tell the truth, if you put it that way—we're actually not doing badly. Working hard gets to be a way of life.

Doctor: A very unhealthy way of life—at least for you.

George: I see your point. It's a problem.

Doctor: If we're going to try doing without the Ativan, I want some commitment from you that you'll try to work on your life-style. You could try limiting the number of accounts that you handle. And you need some time off.

George: All right. As a matter of fact, I'll talk to my wife about it tonight. She's been saying she doesn't see me enough.

Doctor: That sounds like a good start.

George: Then, can I quit the Ativan?

Doctor: Not so fast. You've taken Ativan every day for 4 months, and you need to quit gradually. Here is a schedule to reduce your dose very gradually over the next month.

In the meantime, I want you to think about seeing a counselor. Here's the name of a person who specializes in helping people with high-pressure jobs.

George: Will this be very expensive?

Doctor: Your health insurance will cover most of it.

George: Does this mean I'm crazy?

Doctor: No more than anyone who works in a highly competitive field.

George: All right, Doctor. I'm willing to give it a try.

Doctor: Good. I'll see you in a month for a blood-pressure check. Call me sooner if you need to.

We hope that your doctor is like the second or third ones, educable and willing to be influenced by an informed patient. If so, it will be much easier for you to stop Valium or other benzodiazepines. If the Texas Survey discussed in Chapter 2 is any indication of what goes on in the rest of the country, 10,000 to 20,000 or more patients using Valium-like drugs are treated each year in their doctors' offices for tranquilizer-withdrawal symptoms.

If your doctor is more like the first one—denying the addiction problem and then recommending what amounts to going "cold turkey"—you may need to go to another doctor or to a drug-abuse treatment program. Again, you are not alone. Federally funded drug-abuse treatment centers—listed at the end of this chapter—help more than 7,000 people a year because of problems related to the use of tranquilizers.[2] Those people with tranquilizer-induced medical problems, especially addiction, who are not fortunate enough either to have their own doctor or to find a drug-abuse treatment program may need to go to their nearest hospital emergency room. In 1980, such facilities saw an estimated 8,000 people whose problem was addiction to the Valium family of drugs.[3]

To repeat, if you are having a problem with Valium—or any benzodiazepine—and stopping Valium is stopping you, *you are not alone.* As discussed earlier in this chapter, suddenly stopping a drug like Valium, if you have been using it for more than a month or so, is not a good idea. Tapering your daily dose by an average of 5% to 10% each day (see Scenario B) is much safer.[4] For another example, if you have been using one 5 mg Valium tablet 4 times a day, the first week you might reduce the dose to 1 pill 3 times a day, the second week to 1 pill twice a day, and the third week to 1 pill once a day. The fourth week, you might try one 2 mg pill a day.

Whatever the dose-tapering schedule, it should be worked out with your doctor or other health professional, and you should keep a copy of it with you at all times.

Where to Go for Help

The road back from addiction is not an easy one. If you have decided to stop taking one of the drugs discussed in this book, you will probably need help. Fortunately, help is available, but finding it may require some effort.

Your own physician would be a good person to consult. If he or she is sympathetic and understands the importance of gradual withdrawal, your doctor could be an excellent resource or referral source.

If your physician will not help you or does not seem to know how, you will need to investigate other resources, such as those listed at the end of this chapter.

It may help to have a friend or relative assist you in your search. Be sure to enlist a helper who sincerely wants you to succeed.

This section will explain the steps in stopping drug use, describe how to find the resources available to help you, and suggest how to evaluate available resources, in order to find the ones that will help you the most.

Steps in Stopping Drug Use

If you are addicted to a drug like Valium, you probably already know how hard it is to stop taking the drug, or even to cut down on your dose.

As you know from reading this book, sudden withdrawal could have extremely dangerous consequences, and many people find it difficult to taper off gradually without encouragement and reassurance.

The first step in becoming free of Valium, or any benzodiazepine, is to obtain a professional evaluation to determine the nature and extent of your problem. Such an evaluation, which might be carried out by an expert or by a team of professionals, including a physician, a psychologist, and a social worker, can help you decide upon a course of action. Such an evaluation should suggest a plan of treatment and the resources most suited to your particular needs.

The next step in becoming free of Valium, or any benzodiazepine, is called "detoxification." Detoxification is a term meaning "becoming drug-free." The detoxification process may take weeks or months. It may even require that you stay in a treatment center to assure the availability of necessary support services.

The final step in becoming free of Valium, or any benzodiazepine, consists of a rehabilitation process to help you restructure your life so that you can cope with stress without drugs. Self-help groups, therapy groups, and individual counseling are among the resources that you might consider to help you "get over the rough spots" in your life without the use of benzodiazepines or other addictive drugs.

The kind of help you will need depends upon the severity of your problem.

Perhaps you have a developing addiction problem. The support of a lay self-help group may be sufficient to help you learn to deal with stress without drugs while you gradually cut back your dosage under the supervision of a doctor. The evaluating agency in your community should be able to direct you to local self-help groups appropriate to your needs.

Perhaps you have a more severe addiction problem. You may require treatment in a residential, hospital-based program, where around-the-clock medical support is available, and where frequent individual and group therapy sessions will help you learn to restructure your life without pills. Such programs are often linked with outpatient services and self-help groups that provide ongoing support after residential treatment is completed.

Some of these programs work with other kinds of addiction, including alcoholism. The costs of such programs may be covered by health-insurance policies or certain public benefits. The agency helping you plan your course of treatment can help you to find an appropriate program that fits your financial situation.

How to Find the Resources Available to Help You

A good beginning in seeking safe, effective help in stopping Valium or similar drugs is to contact state or federal agencies established for this purpose.

At the end of this chapter, you will find lists of state agencies and Veterans Administration medical facilities that can help you to locate the people and organizations in your community that provide professional guidance.

A list of National Institute on Drug Abuse community correspondents is also provided. These individuals are engaged chiefly in research, but they may also offer suggestions for locating resources in your area.

Your local mental health organizations may also be a valuable source of information and assistance. Local telephone directories frequently list these under the heading "Mental Health."

The first person you reach at one of these offices may refer you to another office. You may telephone or visit several offices before you find the right one for your needs. Don't give up!

Eventually you will find the person who can help you locate the appropriate resources in your community.

An alternative first step, if you work for a large company, may be to seek advice from your company employee-assistance program.

Increasing numbers of employers, recognizing the expense of recruiting, training, and developing an experienced staff, have seen the value of maintaining employee-assistance programs for employees with personal problems.

If you are thinking about seeking help from the employee-assistance program where you work, it would be wise to check its reputation by speaking with other employees. You should examine a copy of your company policy concerning the employee assistance program to determine what the program has to offer, how eligibility is determined, how employee confidentiality is protected, and how to go about obtaining the services of the program.

Another source of information might be a member of the clergy. Increasingly, religious denominations have responded to the need for reliable information on addiction and have supported members of the clergy in their efforts to help members of their congregations with such problems. Your minister, priest, rabbi, or other religious leader may be able to help you locate sources of professional treatment.

Above all, make sure that the person you choose is well trained and qualified to work with problems of addiction, particularly addiction to Valium and the other benzodiazepines. A counselor with appropriate professional training and background in the treatment of addictive diseases could be very helpful in directing you toward appropriate resources.

Be wary of anyone who urges you to stop taking your pills suddenly, who attempts to substitute another kind of drug for the one to which you are now addicted, or who does not seem to recognize that you have a serious medical problem.

How to Evaluate Available Resources

There is no substitute for common sense. Now that you have read *Stopping Valium,* you know more about the problems of addiction to Valium and other benzodiazepine drugs than many other people, and you should have a good idea of the kinds of questions you would like answered about the people and institutions available to help you.

You will probably want to find out something about the professional backgrounds of the people with whom you are working. Any reputable professional should be willing to tell you about his or her professional training and experience—including degrees, certification, or licensure—in the area of treating addictive disorders. Also find out, however, what standards this person must meet for certification; they vary from one state to another.

If you are referred to an institutional program, whether hospital-based or free-standing, inquire about its state licensure or certification or its accreditation by a private accrediting body. Find out what standards must be met for such approval.

While this will not guarantee an ideal program, it will be a positive step toward obtaining information concerning the capacity of the program to meet your needs.

About Self-Help Groups

Hundreds of self-help groups meet throughout the United States, Canada, and the rest of the world to provide assistance, encouragement, and support to individuals with addiction problems and to their families.

Some groups concentrate on alcoholism, while others focus on addiction to street drugs. While few specialize in prescription-drug addiction, this is a growing area.

Some groups work primarily with women, and others with particular ethnic groups. Some are affiliated with nationwide organizations, while others are set up locally. Community centers, YMCAs, YWCAs, churches, hospitals, and other local organizations may sponsor or house such groups.

Self-help groups can be a great source of support and encouragement for people stopping Valium and other benzodiazepines. Regular meetings, where people share problems and solutions, can be helpful in providing insight and suggesting ways of coping

However, the very strength of self-help groups—lay persons solving problems together—can also be a drawback unless you are simultaneously receiving competent professional advice.

Sometimes individuals involved in self-help groups may not understand the hazards of sudden withdrawal from Valium and other benzodiazepine drugs and may urge you to come to the next meeting "clean" or drug-free while you are still actively addicted. As we have seen, this could be extremely dangerous.

Local chapters of national organizations may vary in their emphasis upon various kinds of addictions. For instance, one group of an organization that works with alcoholics may have many participants who are addicted to Valium or similar drugs and who understand this problem, while another group may have few or no members who understand such addiction.

Self-help groups may be difficult to locate, because meeting locations and telephone numbers may change from time to time. In addition, from one year to the next, new groups may form, while others disband.

The responsible professional or agency planning your course of treatment with you will, if appropriate, help you to locate a self-help group that will best meet your needs.

Drug-Abuse Treatment Programs

State and U.S. Territory Drug-Abuse Treatment Agencies

Alabama

Department of Mental Health
135 South Union Street
Montgomery, AL 36130
(205) 834-4350

Alaska

Department of Health and Social Services
Office of Alcoholism and Drug Abuse
Pouch H-05-F
231 South Franklin
Juneau, AK 99811
(907) 586-6201

Arizona

Drug Abuse Section
Department of Health Services
Division of Behavioral Health Services
2500 East Van Buren
Phoenix, AZ 85008
(602) 255-1238

Arkansas

Arkansas Office on Alcohol and Drug Abuse Prevention
1515 West 7th Avenue, Suite 300
Little Rock, AR 72202
(501) 371-2603

California

Department of Alcohol and Drug Abuse
111 Capitol Mall
Suite 450
Sacramento, CA 95814
(916) 445-1940

Colorado

Alcohol and Drug Abuse Division
Department of Health
4210 East 11th Avenue
Denver, CO 80220
(303) 320-6137

Connecticut

Connecticut Alcohol and Drug Abuse Commission
999 Asylum Avenue, 3rd Floor
Hartford, CT 06105
(203) 566-4145

Delaware

Bureau of Alcoholism and Drug Abuse
Division of Mental Health
1901 North Dupont Highway
Newcastle, DE 19720
(302) 421-6101

District of Columbia

Alcohol and Drug Abuse
Planning Division
601 Indiana Avenue, NW, Suite 500
Washington, DC 20004
(202) 724-5641

Florida

Drug Abuse Program
Mental Health Program Office
1309 Winewood Boulevard
Building 6, Room 163A
Tallahassee, FL 32301
(904) 488-0900

Georgia

Alcohol and Drug Section
Division of Mental Health and Mental Retardation
Georgia Department of Human Resources
618 Ponce de Leon Avenue, NE
Atlanta, GA 30308
(404) 894-4785

Hawaii

Alcohol and Drug Abuse Branch
3627 Kilauea Avenue, Room 405
Honolulu, HI 96816
(808) 734-2263

Idaho

Bureau of Substance Abuse
Department of Health and Welfare
700 West State Street
Boise, ID 83720
(208) 334-4368

Illinois

Illinois Dangerous Drugs Commission
300 North State Street
Suite 1500
Chicago, IL 60610
(312) 822-9860

Indiana

Division of Addiction Services
Department of Mental Health
429 North Pennsylvania Street
Indianapolis, IN 46204
(317) 232-7816

Iowa

Iowa Department of Substance Abuse
Insurance Exchange Building, Suite 202
505 5th Avenue
Des Moines, IA 50319
(515) 281-3641

Kansas

Alcohol and Drug Abuse Services
2700 West Sixth Street
Biddle Building
Topeka, KS 66606
(913) 296-3925

Kentucky

Alcohol and Drug Branch Bureau for Health Services
Department of Human Resources
275 East Main Street
Frankfort, KY 40621
(502) 564-2880

Louisiana

Office of Mental Health and
Substance Abuse
P.O. Box 4049
655 North 5th Street
Baton Rouge, LA 70821
(504) 342-2565

Maine

Office of Alcoholism and Drug
Abuse Prevention
Bureau of Rehabilitation
32 Winthrop Street
Augusta, ME 04330
(207) 289-2781

Maryland

Maryland State Drug Abuse
Administration
201 West Preston Street
Baltimore, MD 21201
(301) 383-3312

Massachusetts

Division of Drug Rehabilitation
160 North Washington Street
Boston, MA 02114
(617) 727-8614

Michigan

Office of Substance Abuse
Services
Department of Public Health
3500 North Logan Street
Lansing, MI 48909
(517) 373-8603

Minnesota

Chemical Dependency Program
Division
Department of Public Welfare
Centennial Building, 4th Floor
658 Cedar Street
St. Paul, MN 55155
(612) 296-4614

Mississippi

Division of Alcohol and Drug
Abuse
Department of Mental Health
Robert E. Lee Office Building,
12th Floor
Jackson, MS 39201
(601) 354-7031

Missouri

Division of Alcoholism and Drug
Abuse
Department of Mental Health
2002 Missouri Boulevard
Jefferson City, MO 65101
(314) 751-4942

Montana

Alcohol and Drug Abuse Division
Department of Institutions
1539 11th Avenue
Helena, MT 59601
(406) 449-2827

Nebraska

Division on Alcoholism and Drug Abuse
Department of Public Institutions
801 West Van Dorn
P.O. Box 94728
Lincoln, NE 68509
(402) 471-2851

Nevada

Bureau of Alcohol and Drug Abuse
Department of Human Resources
505 East King Street
Carson City, NV 89710
(702) 885-4790

New Hampshire

Office of Alcohol and Drug Abuse Prevention
Health and Welfare Building
Hazen Drive
Concord, NH 03301
(603) 271-4627

New Jersey

Division of Narcotic and Drug Abuse Control
129 East Hanover Street
Trenton, NJ 08625
(609) 292-8930

New Mexico

Substance Abuse Bureau
Behavioral Services Division
Health and Environment Department
P.O. Box 968
Santa Fe, NM 87503
(505) 827-5271 ext. 228

New York

Division of Substance Abuse Services
Executive Park South, Box 8200
Albany, NY 12203
(518) 457-7629

New York State Division of Substance Abuse Services
Committee on Prescription Drug Misuse
2 World Trade Center, 67th Floor
New York, NY 10047
(212) 488-4253

North Carolina

Alcohol and Drug Abuse Section
Division of Mental Health and Mental Retardation Services
325 North Salisbury Street
Albermarle Building, Room 1100
Raleigh, NC 27611
(919) 733-4670

North Dakota

Division of Alcoholism and Drug Abuse
Mental Health/Mental Retardation Services
State Department of Health
909 Basin Avenue
Bismarck, ND 58505
(701) 224-2767

Ohio

Bureau of Drug Abuse
65 South Front Street, Suite 211
Columbus, OH 43215
(614) 466-9023

Oklahoma

Alcohol and Drug Programs
Department of Mental Health
4545 North Lincoln Boulevard,
Suite 100, East Terrace
P.O. Box 53277, Capitol Station
Oklahoma City, OK 73152
(405) 521-0044

Oregon

Program for Drug Problems
Mental Health Division
2575 Bittern Street, NE
Salem, OR 97310
(503) 378-2163

Pennsylvania

Office of Drug and Alcohol
Programs
2101 North Front Street
Harrisburg, PA 17120
(717) 787-9857

Rhode Island

Division of Substance Abuse
303 General Hospital
Rhode Island Medical Center
Cranston, RI 02920
(401) 464-2091

South Carolina

Commission on Alcohol and
Drug Abuse
3700 Forest Drive
Landmark East, Suite 300
Columbia, SC 29204
(803) 758-2183

South Dakota

Division of Alcohol and Drug
Abuse
Joe Foss Building
Pierre, SD 57501
(605) 773-4806

Tennessee

Alcohol and Drug Abuse Services
Tennessee Department of Mental
Health and Mental Retardation
James K. Polk Building
505 Deaderick Street
Nashville, TN 37219
(615) 741-1921

Texas

Drug Abuse Prevention Division
Texas Department of Community
Affairs
P.O. Box 13166
Austin, TX 78711
(512) 475-2431

Utah

Division of Alcoholism and
Drugs
150 West North Temple, Suite
350
P.O. Box 2500
Salt Lake City, UT 84110
(801) 533-6532

Vermont

Alcohol and Drug Abuse Division
Department of Social and
Rehabilitation Services
103 South Main Street
Waterbury, VT 05676
(802) 241-2170

Virginia

Division of Substance Abuse
Department of Mental Health and Mental Retardation
P.O. Box 1797
109 Governor Street
Richmond, VA 23214
(804) 786-5313

Washington

Bureau of Alcoholism and Substance Abuse
Washington Department of Social and Health Services
Office Building
Olympia, WA 98504
(206) 753-5866

West Virginia

Division of Alcohol and Drug Abuse
State Capitol
1800 Kanawha Boulevard East
Charleston, WV 25305
(304) 348-3616

Wisconsin

State Bureau of Alcohol and Other Drug Abuse
One West Wilson Street
Madison, WI 53707
(608) 266-2717

Wyoming

Alcohol and Drug Abuse Programs
Hathaway Building, 4th Floor
Cheyenne, WY 82002
(307) 777-7115 ext. 7118

Puerto Rico

Department of Addiction Control Services
P.O. Box B-Y
Piedras Station, PR 00928
(809) 764-8140

American Samoa

Mental Health Clinic
Government of American Samoa
Pago Pago, AS 96799

Guam

Mental Health and Substance Abuse Agency
P.O. Box 20999
Guam, GU 96921
(671) 477-9704

Virgin Islands

Division of Mental Health, Alcoholism and Drug Dependency
P.O. Box 520
Christiansted
St. Croix, VI 00820
(809) 774-4888
(809) 249-7959

Trust Territories

Department of Health Services
Office of the High Commissioner
Saipa, TT 96950
(615) 741-1921

Veterans Administration Hospital Drug-Abuse Treatment Programs

Arizona

VA Medical Center
Drug Dependence Treatment
Program Administration
South Sixth Avenue
Tucson, AZ 85704
(602) 792-1450 ext. 581

Arkansas

VA Medical Center
Drug Dependence Treatment
Program Inpatient
300 East Roosevelt Road,
Building 63,
Room 116E
Little Rock, AR 72206
(501) 372-8361

California

VA Medical Center
Drug Dependence Treatment
Program Administration
5901 East 7th Street, Ward J1,
Building 128
Long Beach, CA 90822
(213) 498-6834 ext. 2834

VA Medical Center
Drug Dependence Treatment
Program Administration
Los Angeles (Brentwood), CA
90073
(213) 478-3711 ext. 2594

VA Medical Center
Drug Dependence Treatment
Program Inpatient
150 Muir Road
Martinez, CA 94553

VA Medical Center
Drug Dependence Treatment
Program Inpatient
3801 Miranda Avenue, Room
116A5-MPD
Menlo Park, CA 94025
(415) 493-5000 ext. 2141

VA Medical Center
Drug Dependence Treatment
Program Inpatient
3801 Miranda Avenue, 4B2
Palo Alto, CA 94304
(415) 493-5000 ext. 5406

VA Medical Center
Drug Dependence Treatment
Program Administration
3350 La Jolla Village Drive
San Diego, CA 92161

VA Satellite
Substance Abuse Treatment
Clinic
4150 Clement Street
San Francisco, CA 94121
(415) 385-8206 ext. 116

VA Medical Center
Drug Dependence Treatment
Program Inpatient
16111 Plummer Street
Sepulveda, CA 91343
(213) 894-8271 ext. 2703

Colorado

VA Medical Center
Drug Dependence Treatment
Program Administration
2222 East 18th Avenue
Denver, CO 80206
(303) 399-8020 ext. 151

District of Columbia

VA Medical Center
Drug Dependence Treatment
Program Outpatient
3120 Georgia Avenue, NW
Washington, DC 20422
(202) 745-8000

VA Medical Center
Drug Dependence Treatment
Program Inpatient
50 Irving Street, NW
Washington, DC 20422
(202) 745-8000

Florida

VA Medical Center
Drug Dependence Treatment
Program Inpatient
1201 NW 16th Street, Room 116F
Miami, FL 33125
(305) 324-4455 ext. 3330

VA Medical Center
Drug Dependence Treatment
Program Outpatient
900 NW Seventh Avenue
Miami, FL 33125
(305) 324-4455 ext. 3578

Georgia

VA Medical Center
Drug Dependence Treatment
Program Outpatient
354 Peachtree Street
Atlanta, GA 30308
(404) 221-5637

VA Medical Center
Drug Dependence Treatment
Program Inpatient
1670 Clairmont Road
Decatur, GA 30033
(404) 321-6111 ext. 451

Illinois

VA Medical Center
Drug Dependence Treatment
Program Inpatient
820 South Damen Avenue, P.O. Box 8195
Chicago, IL 60680
(312) 666-6500 ext. 462

VA Medical Center
Drug Dependence Treatment
Program Administration
Building 53 MP 116C, Room 18
Hines, IL 60141
(312) 261-6700 ext. 2087

VA Medical Center
Drug Dependence Treatment
Program Inpatient
Building 46 D D T C
North Chicago (Downey), IL 60064
(312) 689-1900 ext. 2605

Indiana

VA Medical Center
Drug Dependence Treatment
Program Inpatient
1481 West 10th Street
Indianapolis, IN 46202
(317) 635-7401

Louisiana

VA Medical Center
Drug Dependence Treatment
Program Inpatient
1601 Perdido Street
New Orleans, LA 70140
(504) 568-0811 ext. 251

VA Medical Center
Drug Dependence Treatment
Program Outpatient
639 South Rendon
New Orleans, LA 70119
(504) 821-5466

Maryland

VA Medical Center
Drug Dependence Treatment
Program Inpatient
3900 Loch Raven Boulevard
Baltimore, MD 21218
(301) 467-9932 ext. 5368

Massachusetts

VA Medical Center
Drug Dependence Treatment
Program Inpatient
200 Springs Road
Bedford, MA 01730
(617) 275-7500 ext. 561

VA Medical Center
Drug Dependence Treatment
Program Inpatient
150 South Huntington Avenue
Boston, MA 02130
(617) 232-9500 ext. 451

VA Medical Center
Drug Dependence Treatment
Program Outpatient
125 Lincoln Street
Boston, MA 02111
(617) 223-4571

VA Medical Center
Alcohol and Drug Dependence
Program
Brockton, MA 02401
(617) 583-4500 ext. 494

Michigan

VA Medical Center
Drug Dependence Treatment
Program Inpatient
Allen Park, MI 48101
(800) 555-1212

VA Medical Center
Drug Dependence Treatment
Program Inpatient
Room 116E
Battle Creek, MI 49016
(616) 965-3281 ext. 661

Minnesota

VA Medical Center
Drug Dependence Treatment
Program Administration
54th Street and 48th Avenue
South
Minneapolis, MN 55417
(612) 725-6767 ext. 6866

Missouri

VA Medical Center
Drug Dependence Treatment
Program Inpatient
Jefferson Barracks
St. Louis, MO 63125
(314) 487-0400 ext. 451

New Jersey

VA Medical Center
Drug Dependence Treatment
Program Inpatient
Tremont Avenue
East Orange, NJ 07019
(201) 676-1000

New York

VA Medical Center
Drug Dependence Treatment
Program Inpatient
113 Holland Avenue
Albany, NY 12208
(518) 462-3311 ext. 522

VA Medical Center
Drug Dependence Treatment
Program Inpatient
130 West Kingsbridge Road
Bronx, NY 10468
(212) 584-9000 ext. 583

VA Medical Center
Drug Dependence Treatment
Program Administration
800 Poly Place
Brooklyn, NY 11209
(212) 836-6600 ext. 425

VA Medical Center
Drug Dependence Treatment
Program Inpatient
3495 Bailey Avenue
Buffalo, NY 14215
(716) 834-9200 ext. 295

VA Medical Center
Drug Dependence Treatment
Program Inpatient
Building 52B
Montrose, NY 10548
(914) 737-4400 ext. 213

VA Medical Center
Drug Dependence Treatment
Program Inpatient
First Avenue at East 24th Street
New York, NY 10010
(212) 686-7500 ext. 755

Ohio

VA Medical Center
Drug Dependence Treatment
Program Administration
3200 Vine Street
Cincinnati, OH 45220
(513) 861-3100 ext. 4775

VAMC Wade Park
Drug Dependence Treatment
Program Outpatient
10000 Brecksville Road

Cleveland, OH 44141
(216) 791-3800 ext. 7534

VA Medical Center
Drug Dependence Treatment
Program Administration
10000 Brecksville Road
Cleveland, OH 44141
(216) 526-3030 ext. 351

Pennsylvania

VA Medical Center
Drug Dependence Treatment
Program Inpatient
Building 11
Coatesville, PA 19320
(215) 384-7711 ext. 477

VA Medical Center
Drug Dependence Treatment
Program Administration
University and Woodland
Avenues
Philadelphia, PA 19104
(215) 382-2400 ext. 468

VA Medical Center
Drug Dependence Treatment
Program Inpatient
University Drive
Pittsburgh, PA 15224
(412) 683-3000 ext. 421

VA Medical Center
Drug Dependence Treatment
Program Outpatient
5108 Baum Boulevard
Pittsburgh, PA 15224
(412) 683-3000 ext. 421

Oklahoma

VA Medical Center
Drug Dependence Treatment
Program Administration
921 NE 13th Street
Oklahoma City, OK 73104
(465) 272-9876

VA Satellite
Drug Dependence Treatment
Program Outpatient
1717 North Pedria
Tulsa, OK 74106
(918) 585-8207

Rhode Island

VA Medical Center
Drug Dependence Treatment
Program Outpatient
Davis Park
Providence, RI 02908
(401) 273-7100 ext. 357

Tennessee

VA Medical Center
Drug Dependence Treatment
Program Inpatient
1030 Jefferson Avenue
Memphis, TN 38104
(901) 523-8990

VA Medical Center
Drug Dependence Treatment
Program Outpatient
1030 Jefferson Avenue
Memphis, TN 38104
(901) 523-8990

Texas

VA Medical Center
Drug Dependence Treatment
Program Administration
4500 South Lancaster Road
Dallas, TX 75216
(214) 376-5451 ext. 338

VA Medical Center
Drug Dependence Treatment
Program Inpatient
2002 Holcombe Boulevard
Houston, TX 77211
(713) 747-3000

Utah

VA Medical Center
Drug Dependence Treatment
Program Inpatient
500 Foothill Boulevard
Salt Lake City, UT 84148
(801) 582-1565 ext. 1870

VA Medical Center
Drug Dependence Treatment
Program SATE
820 East 400 South
Salt Lake City, UT 84102
(801) 582-1565 ext. 1155

Virginia

VA Medical Center
Drug Dependence Treatment
Program Inpatient
1201 Broad Rock Road
Richmond, VA 23219
(804) 233-9631 ext. 208

Washington

VA Medical Center
Drug Dependence Treatment
Program Administration
4435 Beacon Avenue
Seattle, WA 98108
(206) 622-4081

VA Medical Center
Drug Dependence Treatment
Program Inpatient
American Lake
Tacoma, WA 98493
(206) 582-8440 ext. 6110

VA Medical Center
Drug Dependence Treatment
Program Administration
4th Plain and "O" Streets
Vancouver, WA 98661
(206) 696-4061 ext. 226

Wisconsin

VA Medical Center
Drug Dependence Treatment
Program Inpatient
5000 West National Avenue
Wood, WI 53193
(414) 384-2000 ext. 2463

Puerto Rico

VA Medical Center
Drug Dependence Treatment
Program
GPO Box 4867
San Juan, PR 00936
(809) 764-4545 ext. 590

National Institute on Drug Abuse Community Correspondents Groups: Resources for Further Information on Drug Abuse

California

Balkar Husson, Ph.D.
Patient Management and Needs Assessment
Los Angeles County Office of Drug Abuse
849 South Broadway, 11th Floor
Los Angeles, CA 90012
(213) 974-7181

Dennis McCartin
Research Analyst
San Diego County Department of Health Services
Division of Drug Programs
2870 4th Avenue
San Diego, CA 92103
(714) 236-2200

John Newmeyer, Ph.D.
Epidemiologist
Haight-Ashbury Free Medical Clinics
529 Clayton Street
San Francisco, CA 94117
(415) 621-2015

Colorado

Robert Booth, Ph.D.
Program Planning and Evaluation
Alcohol and Drug Division
State of Colorado Department of Health
4210 East 11th Avenue
Denver, CO 80220
(303) 320-6137 ext. 368

District of Columbia

George Powell
Chief
Central Intake Division
Alcohol and Drug Abuse Service Administration
1400 Q Street, NW, 3rd Floor
Washington, DC 20009
(202) 673-6638

Florida

James Rivers, Ph.D.
Health Services Research Center
Medical Arts Building, Room 309
1550 NW 10th Avenue
Miami, FL 33136
(305) 547-6005

Georgia

James Delaney
Compliance Coordinator
Alcohol and Drug Services Section
Division of Mental Health and Mental Retardation
State of Georgia Department of Human Services
618 Ponce de Leon Avenue, NE
Atlanta, GA 30308
(404) 894-3784

Illinois

Wayne Wiebel
Research Sociologist
State of Illinois Dangerous Drug Commission
300 North State Street, Suite 1502
Chicago, IL 60610
(312) 822-9860 ext. 255

Louisiana

Gail Thornton
Public Health Educator
New Orleans Health Department
1545 Tulane Avenue, 2nd Floor
New Orleans, LA 70112
(504) 586-4934

Massachusetts

Craig Lambert, Ph.D.
Director of Research and Evaluation
Division of Preventive Medicine
Massachusetts Department of Public Health
600 Washington Street, Room 705
Boston, MA 02111
(617) 727-7170

Michigan

Richard Caulkins
Licensing, Evaluation and Data Service
Office of Substance Abuse
P.O. Box 30035
Lansing, MI 48909
(517) 373-8358

Minnesota

Bruce Hutchinson
Research Coordinator
Chemical Dependency Program Division
Department of Public Welfare
Centennial Building, 4th Floor
658 Cedar Street
St. Paul, MN 55155
(612) 296-4612

Missouri

Alphonse Poklis, Ph.D.
Department of Pathology
St. Louis University School of Medicine
1402 South Grand
St. Louis, MO 63104
(314) 727-6300

New Jersey

John French
Chief, Research and Evaluation
Division of Narcotics and Drug Abuse Control
State of New Jersey Department of Health
129 East Hanover Street
Trenton, NJ 08608
(609) 292-8930

New York

Nathaniel Webster, M.D.
Erie County Medical Center
462 Grider Street
Buffalo, NY 14215
(716) 898-3625

Blanche Frank, Ph.D.
Chief, Epidemiology Unit
State of New York Division of
Substance Abuse Services
2 World Trade Center,
67th Floor
New York, NY 10047
(212) 488-3967

Pennsylvania

Christopher D'Amanda, M.D.
Addiction Services Medical
Director
Coordinating Office for Drug
and Alcohol Abuse Programs
City of Philadelphia Department
of Public Health
841 Chestnut Street, 3rd Floor
Philadelphia, PA 19107
(215) 592-5417

Texas

Roy Griffin
Health Planning Associate
Texas Area V HSA
610 South Industrial Boulevard
Suite 220
Euless, TX 76039
(817) 540-1800

Washington

Charles Ball
Director, Planning and
Evaluation
King County Department of
Public Health
Division of Alcoholism and
Substance Abuse Services
1008 Smith Tower
2nd Avenue and Yesler
Seattle, WA 98104
(206) 344-7635

The National Institute on Drug Abuse also publishes the National Directory of Drug Abuse Treatment Programs, which lists approximately 3,500 drug-abuse treatment centers in the United States and its territories. Single copies of this directory are available free of charge from: National Clearinghouse for Drug Abuse Information, P.O. Box 416, Kensington, MD 20795.

[From Medical Aspects of Human Sexuality, December 1969]

Old Style (Late 1960's) Advertisement for Tranquilizer

You can't set her free. But you can help her feel less anxious.

You know this woman.

She's anxious, tense, irritable. She's felt this way for months.

Beset by the seemingly insurmountable problems of raising a young family, and confined to the home most of the time, her symptoms reflect a sense of inadequacy and isolation. Your reassurance and guidance may have helped some, but not enough.

SERAX (oxazepam) cannot change her environment, of course. But it can help relieve anxiety, tension, agitation and irritability, thus strengthening her ability to cope with day-to-day problems. Eventually—as she regains confidence and composure—your counsel may be all the support she needs.

> Indicated in anxiety, tension, agitation, irritability, and anxiety associated with depression.
>
> May be used in a broad range of patients, generally with considerable dosage flexibility.

IN BRIEF.

Contraindications: History of previous hypersensitivity to oxazepam. Oxazepam is not indicated in psychoses.

Warning: *Use in Pregnancy:* Safety for use in pregnancy not established.

Precautions: Hypotensive reactions are rare, but use with caution where complications could ensue from a fall in blood pressure, especially in the elderly. Withdrawal symptoms upon discontinuation have been noted in some patients exhibiting drug dependence through chronic overdose. Carefully supervise dose and amounts prescribed, especially for patients prone to self-overdose; excessive, prolonged use in susceptible patients (alcoholics, ex-addicts, etc.) may result in dependence or habituation. Reduce dosage gradually after prolonged excessive dosage to avoid possible epileptiform seizures. Withdrawal symptoms following abrupt discontinuance are similar to those seen with barbiturates. Caution patients against driving or operating machinery until absence of drowsiness or dizziness is ascertained. Warn patients of possible reduction in alcohol tolerance.
Not indicated in children under 6 years; absolute dosage for 6- to 12-year-olds not established.

Adverse Reactions: Therapy-interrupting side effects are rare. Transient mild drowsiness is common initially; if persistent, reduce dosage. Dizziness, vertigo and headache have also occurred infrequently; syncope, rarely. Mild paradoxical reactions (excitement, stimulation of affect) are reported in psychiatric patients. Minor diffuse rashes (morbilliform, urticarial and maculopapular) are rare. Nausea, lethargy, edema, slurred speech, tremor and altered libido are rare and generally controllable by dosage reduction. Although rare, leukopenia and hepatic dysfunction including jaundice have been reported during therapy. Periodic blood counts and liver function tests are advised. Ataxia, reported rarely, does not appear related to dose or age. These side reactions, noted with related compounds, are not yet reported: paradoxical excitation with severe rage reactions, hallucinations, menstrual irregularities, change in EEG pattern, blood dyscrasias (including agranulocytosis), blurred vision, diplopia, incontinence, stupor, disorientation, fever and euphoria.

Availability: Capsules of 10, 15 and 30 mg. oxazepam; tablets of 15 mg. oxazepam.

To help you relieve anxiety and tension

Serax®
(oxazepam)

Wyeth®
SERVICE TO MEDICINE

Wyeth Laboratories
Philadelphia, Pa.

6

Drug Companies Push Valium and Its Cousins to Your Doctor—Who Pushes Them to You

A beautiful white bird flying over a shiny silver metallic model of a human brain.[1]

The gold-braceleted hand of an elegant woman, extinguishing a cigarette in a white china ashtray.[2]

A large "pullout" card, rather like a large novelty birthday card for a very young child, featuring half a dozen red, yellow, and blue hexagonal nuts (representing a chemical configuration) trailed by colorful ribbon streamers.[3]

What do all of these have in common?

These are the pictures that your doctor has probably already seen many times in medical-journal and direct-mail advertisements reminding him to prescribe Valium and its cousins for his patients.

Women who read fashion magazines or who have charge accounts at high-quality department stores will recognize the style of these advertisements. They are reminiscent of fashion advertisements and flyers for expensive lines of cosmetics.

Preposterous? Apparently the drug companies do not consider it so, for they willingly spend millions of dollars each year to promote drugs in exactly this way. In 1978, for example, Hoffmann-LaRoche spent $35 million promoting its products, particularly its best-selling benzodiazepines, Valium, Librium, and Dalmane.[4] Over two-thirds of this was spent on medical-journal and direct-mail advertising to physicians.

Colorful, multi-page spreads in medical journals, elaborate folders sent in the mail, and armies of salespeople making individual visits to physicians are included in the daily informational barrage emanating from huge drug companies to make sure that your doctor doesn't forget to write you a prescription for one or more of the company's line of products.

But doesn't everybody advertise? Of course. However, advertisements for most consumer goods are aimed at the people who purchase and use the product. Advertising for prescription drugs, on the other hand, is customarily directed only toward physicians. Thus, advertisements convince your doctor to prescribe drugs such as Valium, but you are the one who will use the drug and pay for it, and for the expensive advertising as well.

You also pay when your doctor, who has been subtly (or not so subtly) influenced by professional advertising, prescribes a drug that is not good for you.

Because *you* are the one who will pay for and use the product, and because your dollars also pay for the expensive advertising, you should know what your doctor sees in the medical journals, receives in the mail, and hears from drug-company salespeople who call at his or her office.

A major effect of modern drug advertising is to drive home to both physicians and lay people (reaching the latter through nonprescription drug advertising and "public service" advertising) the so-called "pain-pill-pleasure"

New Style (Early 1980's) Advertisement for Tranquilizer

Schering Introduces
Measurable
PEACE OF MIND

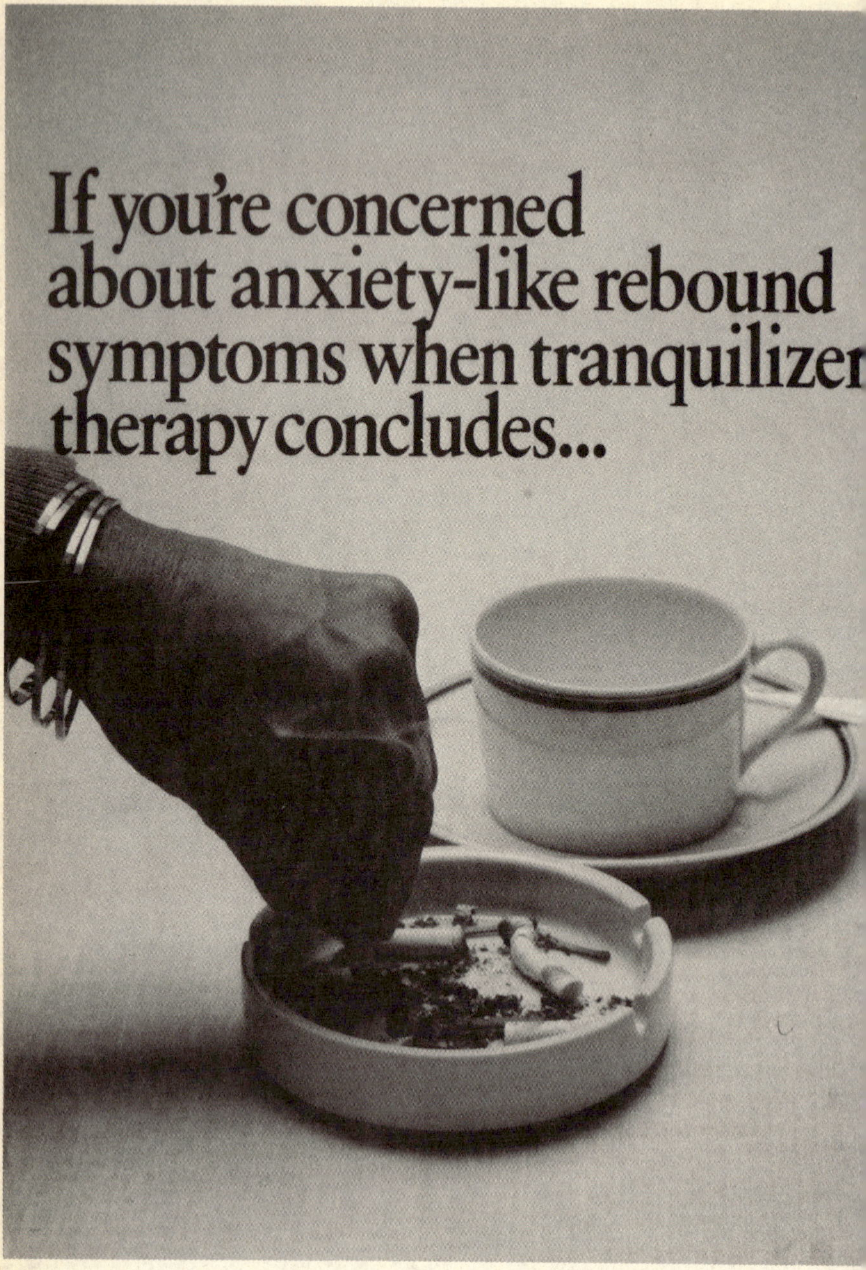
If you're concerned
about anxiety-like rebound
symptoms when tranquilizer
therapy concludes...

-mg, 5-mg, 10-mg scored tablets

VALIUM® (IV)

diazepam/Roche

PULL

principle. This is the notion that for every ill or discomfort, whether physical or emotional, there is a drug that will bring relief. By means of a constant onslaught of direct and indirect sales pressure upon the medical profession and general public, drug manufacturers have firmly established the pain-pill-pleasure principle in American medical mythology.

As we saw in chapters 2 and 3, Valium and its cousins are potentially dangerous and addictive. The reason for their enormous sales in the face of these hazards is found, in part, in the economics of medical practice, as well as in the marketing activities of the major drug companies.

To the physician, time is money. No additional money comes in during a lengthy office visit; but the rent, utility bills, salaries of office personnel, insurance premiums, and other expenses continue to mount. Therefore, your doctor may not be able to afford to spend much time talking with you about aspects of your life that are troubling you. He may not refer you to counseling, either because he does not know too much about this himself or because he does not think you would accept it. Thus, he frequently winds up the visit in the "time-honored way"—by writing a prescription. This is the cue for you to leave, satisfied that the doctor has "done something" to help you. In fact, many patients have come to expect this, even though prescription drugs may not be the best solution for their physical or emotional problems. It takes an understanding physician to spend the time and make the effort to explain to a patient that a prescription is not the cure for every ill.

Both patients and doctors need to keep this in mind; both must learn to expect that visits to the doctor need not be terminated with the prescription-writing ritual.

Physicians who are comfortable doing so may help their patients a great deal just by listening to their concerns. All physicians should be familiar with counseling services in the community that are within the financial reach of the patients they serve.

But not all the blame for "problem prescribing" should be placed at the doorstep of impatient physicians and "prescription-seeking" patients.

Drug Promotion—A Lifetime Proposition

From the day they enter medical school until the day they lock their office door behind them for the last time, doctors are the targets of lavishly funded, scientifically executed marketing campaigns by the large drug companies.

Major pharmaceutical houses give gifts and research grants to medical schools. They also freely distribute to medical students various promotional materials designed to keep the name of the company firmly fixed in the budding doctor's mind.

Thus, a student may first listen to a patient's heart with a stethoscope provided by Eli Lilly and Company. He or she may learn to recognize the different heart sounds by listening to tape recordings from the school library, featuring the various sounds made by the healthy and diseased human heart, interspersed with the words "Merck Sharp and Dohme" at frequent intervals.[5]

He or she may study with the aid of a series of well-illustrated handbooks on various medical subjects, a gift from the Upjohn Company, or look up strange new words in a medical dictionary from Sandoz, Inc.[6]

When the young doctor is in the last years of medical school and begins practical training, he or she may enjoy anything from pocket notebooks from CIBA Pharmaceutical Company to doughnuts and pizza parties provided by other drug companies. All of this helps to create a favorable image of the drug company in the mind of the young doctor.

The hard sell does not really begin until the medical student graduates and becomes an intern or resident in charge of the care of many patients in a large teaching hospital. At this point, although they are still supervised by other residents and senior attending physicians, young doctors make many medical decisions independently.

Drug companies have been quick to take advantage of this opportunity to boost sales while influencing the prescribing habits of young doctors. Platoons of drug-company salespeople (known in the industry as detailmen) are dispatched to teaching hospitals to promote the use of their company's products among the interns and resident staff.

According to Dr. Quentin Young, former chairman of the Department of Medicine at Chicago's huge Cook County Hospital, the "hospital had been turned into a very high-pressure bazaar" by drug company detailmen working the corridors.

In 1975, Dr. Young banned drug salesmen from the Department of Medicine at Cook County Hospital. He also issued orders limiting the prescribing of tranquilizing drugs by the house staff. Instead of being free to prescribe such drugs at their discretion, house staff physicians working in the hospital's general-medicine clinic were instructed in the appropriate uses of these drugs. As a result, the number of prescriptions for tranquilizers dropped dramatically, with as much as a two-thirds reduction in the use of some psychoactive drugs.[7] Far from being unhappy with this change, both physicians and patients were generally satisfied with the results.[8]

Physicians trained at Cook County Hospital since 1975 have thus had an opportunity to learn how to practice without relying on Valium and its cousins as a "crutch."

But what about other doctors?

Most doctors receive little formal training in the pharmacology of psychoactive drugs (such as Valium), and most of what they learn about them comes from sources originating within the drug industry. Advertising in medical journals, direct-mail advertisements, and conversations with drug-company salespeople or detailmen are the principal sources of information about tranquilizers for many doctors. Although they can receive more accurate information from recent textbooks, articles in the better medical journals, and consultations with physicians knowledgeable about these drugs, busy doctors may find the drug-company sources much more accessible.

Even if a doctor makes a special effort to keep up by reading medical journals and attending professional meetings in a particular field, he or she will not escape the pervasive promotional influence of the drug manufacturers.

As psychiatrist Natalie Shainess told the United States Senate Subcommittee on Monopoly of the Select Committee on Small Business in 1971, regarding the activities of drug companies in the field of psychiatry: "There is virtually no meeting, no publication, no event that is not funded in part or in whole by the drug companies."[9]

Most doctors subscribe to at least 2 or 3 medical journals, which are issued at least monthly, and for which they pay. Many doctors subscribe to more. However, virtually every practicing physician in the United States also receives a glut of unsolicited literature, which may amount to hundreds of pieces of mail each week. This paper torrent includes many so-called "throwaway" journals. These are periodicals completely supported by drug advertising, with some editorial copy interspersed among the many pages of advertisements. The doctor's mailbox is also filled to the brim each day with direct-mail advertisements from the major drug companies.

Companies that produce throwaway journals fund

these publications almost entirely through advertising revenues. Some of the throwaways carry articles that may be reasonably informative but tend to be much less objective in articles discussing drugs or the drug industry than they are in articles that do not involve prescription drugs.

The principal purpose of these articles is to attract the attention of the physician to the drug advertisements liberally distributed throughout the publication.

The medical journals that physicians pay to receive are generally of much higher quality than the throwaway journals. They characteristically contain several major articles on recent medical research findings and shorter articles and letters describing specific cases. While these journals may contain proportionally less advertising than the throwaway journals, they too have many pages of drug advertisements. Even though such paid-circulation journals provide important channels of communication for major medical discoveries and are far more independent than the throwaways, they would be badly affected by a loss of drug-advertising revenue. An exception to this is a publication such as *The Medical Letter,* which contains *no* advertising and is therefore viewed by those in the profession as being completely independent.

All of this in turn leads to some serious unanswered questions—first, about the power of a medical journal to refuse false or misleading drug advertising; and second, about the influence drug-advertising revenue (or fear of its loss) might have upon the editorial content of a journal.

Drug companies also use elaborately categorized mailing lists to inundate physicians with direct-mail advertising about products in their practice specialty. Some of these mailings are extensive—and expensive—brochures containing information about specific conditions, with only limited advertising for a specific drug, while others contain lengthy dissertations about the claimed properties and advantages of a specific product in various medical situations.

Are doctors really influenced by all this advertising? While many of the throwaway journals and direct-mail advertisements are destined to be thrown unread into the trash, surveys and polls carried out by drug manufacturers have apparently demonstrated that they produce sales revenues that easily justify their costs.

The fanciful drawings found in many current advertisements for Valium and its cousins would leave most readers with no idea of what type of product was being promoted. The professional labeling—the text approved by the FDA, setting forth the technical information about the proper use of the drug—is generally set in minuscule type, and frequently is not even printed on the same page as the graphic portion of the advertisement.

Yet surveys done by and for drug-advertising agencies have shown that these colorful ads tend to capture doctors' interest and fix the product name in their minds, so that when they are deciding how to treat you, it seems easy and natural for them to prescribe that product.

Advertisements for Valium and its cousins have changed a great deal in the past 15 years. Some of this change has resulted from internal marketing decisions (due in part to unfavorable public response to certain lines of advertising), while other changes have resulted from government oversight regarding drug labeling and advertising.

The Evolution of Tranquilizer Advertising

During the late 1960s and early 1970s, Valium and its cousins were heavily advertised for use in coping with the

APPENDIX II

ADVERTISEMENTS

[From the Journal of the American College Health Association, June 1969, Vol. 17, No. 5]

to help free her of excessive anxiety...

adjunctive Librium®
(chlordiazepoxide HCl)

When mounting pressures combine to threaten the emotional stability of the anxious student, adjunctive use of Librium (chlordiazepoxide HCl) can help relieve the symptoms caused by her excessive anxiety. Together with your counseling and reassurance, Librium, if indicated, can help the anxious student to handle the primary problem and to "get her back on her feet."

On proper maintenance dosage, Librium quickly helps control anxiety and relax emotional tension—usually without impairing mental acuity. The student is thus enabled to direct her youthful energy more efficiently into productive channels...to cope more successfully with her day-to-day problems.

Before prescribing, please consult complete product information, a summary of which follows:

Indications: Indicated when anxiety, tension and apprehension are significant components of the clinical profile.

Contraindications: Patients with known hypersensitivity to the drug.

Warnings: Caution patients about possible combined effects with alcohol and other CNS depressants. As with all CNS-acting drugs, caution patients against hazardous occupations requiring complete mental alertness (*e.g.*, operating machinery, driving). Though physical and psychological dependence have rarely been reported on recommended doses, use caution in administering to addiction-prone individuals or those who might increase dosage; withdrawal symptoms (including convulsions), following discontinuation of the drug and similar to those seen with barbiturates, have been reported. Use of any drug in pregnancy, lactation, or in women of childbearing age requires that its potential benefits be weighed against its possible hazards.

Precautions: In the elderly and debilitated, and in children over six, limit to smallest effective dosage (initially 10 mg or less per day) to preclude ataxia or oversedation, increasing gradually as needed and tolerated. Not recommended in children under six. Though generally not recommended, if combination therapy with other psychotropics seems indicated, carefully consider individual pharmacologic effects, particularly in use of potentiating drugs such as MAO inhibitors and phenothiazines. Observe usual precautions in presence of impaired renal or hepatic function. Paradoxical reactions (*e.g.*, excitement, stimulation and acute rage) have been reported in psychiatric patients and hyperactive aggressive children. Employ usual precautions in treatment of anxiety states with evidence of impending depression; suicidal tendencies may be present and protective measures necessary. Variable effects on blood coagulation have been reported very rarely in patients receiving the drug and oral anticoagulants; causal relationship has not been established clinically.

Adverse Reactions: Drowsiness, ataxia and confusion may occur, especially in the elderly and debilitated. These are reversible in most instances by proper dosage adjustment, but are also occasionally observed at the lower dosage ranges. In a few instances syncope has been reported. Also encountered are isolated instances of skin eruptions, edema, minor menstrual irregularities, nausea and constipation, extrapyramidal symptoms, increased and decreased libido—all infrequent and generally controlled with dosage reduction; changes in EEG patterns (low-voltage fast activity) may appear during and after treatment; blood dyscrasias (including agranulocytosis), jaundice and hepatic dysfunction have been reported occasionally, making periodic blood counts and liver function tests advisable during protracted therapy.

Roche
LABORATORIES
Division of Hoffmann-La Roche Inc.
Nutley, New Jersey 07110

Librium® (chlordiazepoxide HCl) Capsules—5 mg, 10 mg and 25 mg

[From Medical Aspects of Human Sexuality, December 1969]

Old Style (Late 1960's) Advertisement for Tranquilizer

You can't set her free. But you can help her feel less anxious.

You know this woman.

She's anxious, tense, irritable. She's felt this way for months.

Beset by the seemingly insurmountable problems of raising a young family, and confined to the home most of the time, her symptoms reflect a sense of inadequacy and isolation. Your reassurance and guidance may have helped some, but not enough.

SERAX (oxazepam) cannot change her environment, of course. But it can help relieve anxiety, tension, agitation and irritability, thus strengthening her ability to cope with day-to-day problems. Eventually—as she regains confidence and composure—your counsel may be all the support she needs.

> Indicated in anxiety, tension, agitation, irritability, and anxiety associated with depression.
>
> May be used in a broad range of patients, generally with considerable dosage flexibility.

IN BRIEF.

Contraindications: History of previous hypersensitivity to oxazepam. Oxazepam is not indicated in psychoses.

Warning: *Use in Pregnancy:* Safety for use in pregnancy not established.

Precautions: Hypotensive reactions are rare, but use with caution where complications could ensue from a fall in blood pressure, especially in the elderly. Withdrawal symptoms upon discontinuation have been noted in some patients exhibiting drug dependence through chronic overdose. Carefully supervise dose and amounts prescribed, especially for patients prone to self-overdose; excessive, prolonged use in susceptible patients (alcoholics, ex-addicts, etc.) may result in dependence or habituation. Reduce dosage gradually after prolonged excessive dosage to avoid possible epileptiform seizures. Withdrawal symptoms following abrupt discontinuance are similar to those seen with barbiturates. Caution patients against driving or operating machinery until absence of drowsiness or dizziness is ascertained. Warn patients of possible reduction in alcohol tolerance.
Not indicated in children under 6 years; absolute dosage for 6- to 12-year-olds not established.

Adverse Reactions: Therapy-interrupting side effects are rare. Transient mild drowsiness is common initially; if persistent, reduce dosage. Dizziness, vertigo and headache have also occurred infrequently; syncope, rarely. Mild paradoxical reactions (excitement, stimulation of affect) are reported in psychiatric patients. Minor diffuse rashes (morbilliform, urticarial and maculopapular) are rare. Nausea, lethargy, edema, slurred speech, tremor and altered libido are rare and generally controllable by dosage reduction. Although rare, leukopenia and hepatic dysfunction including jaundice have been reported during therapy. Periodic blood counts and liver function tests are advised. Ataxia, reported rarely, does not appear related to dose or age. These side reactions, noted with related compounds, are not yet reported: paradoxical excitation with severe rage reactions, hallucinations, menstrual irregularities, change in EEG pattern, blood dyscrasias (including agranulocytosis), blurred vision, diplopia, incontinence, stupor, disorientation, fever and euphoria.

Availability: Capsules of 10, 15 and 30 mg. oxazepam; tablets of 15 mg. oxazepam.

To help you relieve anxiety and tension

Serax®
(oxazepam)

Wyeth® SERVICE TO MEDICINE

Wyeth Laboratories
Philadelphia, Pa.

[From the New England Journal of Medicine, October 29, 1970, Vol. 283, No. 18]

Symbols in a life of psychic tension

M.A.

class of '66

Ph.D.

thesis...in progress

G.I.

series and complete examination normal

(persistent indigestion)

Rx

Valium® (diazepam) *t.i.d.* and *h.s.*

M. A. (class of '66)... Ph.D. (thesis, in progress)... letters that represent a young lifetime of work... a formal education nearing completion. But there are still long, arduous examinations to pass, a doctoral thesis to finish... a period in which stress is often converted into the gastrointestinal symptoms of psychic tension. For this kind of patient—with no demonstrable pathology—consider the usefulness of Valium (diazepam).

Valium can help relieve psychic tension and resultant somatic symptoms, within the first day for some patients. Valium is also useful in psychic tension with associated depressive symptoms. And Valium can help relieve psychic tension-induced insomnia with an *h.s.* dose added to the *t.i.d.* schedule.

Valium is generally well tolerated. In proper maintenance dosage it seldom dulls the senses or interferes with functioning. Side effects most commonly reported have been drowsiness, fatigue and ataxia.

Before prescribing, please consult complete product information, a summary of which follows:

Indications: Tension and anxiety states; somatic complaints which are concomitants of emotional factors; psychoneurotic states manifested by tension, anxiety, apprehension, fatigue, depressive symptoms or agitation; acute agitation, tremor, delirium tremens and hallucinosis due to acute alcohol withdrawal; adjunctively in skeletal muscle spasm due to reflex spasm to local pathology, spasticity caused by upper motor neuron disorders, athetosis, stiff-man syndrome, convulsive disorders (not for sole therapy).

Contraindicated: Known hypersensitivity to the drug. Children under 6 months of age. Acute narrow angle glaucoma.

Warnings: Not of value in psychotic patients. Caution against hazardous occupations requiring complete mental alertness. When used adjunctively in convulsive disorders, possibility of increase in frequency and/or severity of grand mal seizures may require increased dosage of standard anticonvulsant medication; abrupt withdrawal may be associated with temporary increase in frequency and/or severity of seizures. Advise against simultaneous ingestion of alcohol and other CNS depressants. Withdrawal symptoms have occurred following abrupt discontinuance. Keep addiction-prone individuals under careful surveillance because of their predisposition to habituation and dependence. In pregnancy, lactation or women of childbearing age, weigh potential benefit against possible hazard.

Precautions: If combined with other psychotropics or anticonvulsants, consider carefully pharmacology of agents employed. Usual precautions indicated in patients severely depressed, or with latent depression, or with suicidal tendencies. Observe usual precautions in impaired renal or hepatic function. Limit dosage to smallest effective amount in elderly and debilitated to preclude ataxia or oversedation.

Side Effects: Drowsiness, confusion, diplopia, hypotension, changes in libido, nausea, fatigue, depression, dysarthria, jaundice, skin rash, ataxia, constipation, headache, incontinence, changes in salivation, slurred speech, tremor, vertigo, urinary retention, blurred vision. Paradoxical reactions such as acute hyperexcited states, anxiety, hallucinations, increased muscle spasticity, insomnia, rage, sleep disturbances, stimulation, have been reported; should these occur, discontinue drug. Isolated reports of neutropenia, jaundice; periodic blood counts and liver function tests advisable during long-term therapy.

Valium® (diazepam)

2-mg, 5-mg, 10-mg tablets

to help relieve psychic tension and its somatic symptoms

[From the New England Journal of Medicine, June 25, 1970, Vol. 282, No. 26]

Symbols in a life of psychic tension

M.A.
(Fine Arts)

PTA
(President-elect)

GYN
repeated examinations normal

(persistent complaints)

Rx

Valium® (diazepam) *t.i.d.* and *h.s.*

M.A. (Fine Arts)... PTA (President-elect)... representations of a life currently centered around home and children, with too little time to pursue a vocation for which she has spent many years in training... a situation that may bespeak continuous frustration and stress: a perfect framework for her to translate the functional symptoms of psychic tension into major problems. For this kind of patient—with no demonstrable pathology yet with repeated complaints—consider the distinctive properties of Valium® (diazepam). Valium possesses a pronounced calming action that usually relieves psychic tension promptly, helping to attenuate the related somatic signs and symptoms. Valium is generally well tolerated. On proper maintenance dosage, Valium seldom dulls the senses or interferes with functioning.

When an *h.s.* dose is added to the *t.i.d.* schedule, Valium helps counter sleeplessness due to psychic tension.

Before prescribing, please consult complete product information, a summary of which follows:

Indications: Tension and anxiety states; somatic complaints which are concomitants of emotional factors; psychoneurotic states manifested by tension, anxiety, apprehension, fatigue, depressive symptoms or agitation; acute agitation, tremor, delirium tremens and hallucinosis due to acute alcohol withdrawal; adjunctively in skeletal muscle spasm due to reflex spasm to local pathology, spasticity caused by upper motor neuron disorders, athetosis, stiff-man syndrome, convulsive disorders (not for sole therapy).

Contraindicated: Known hypersensitivity to the drug. Children under 6 months of age. Acute narrow angle glaucoma.

Warnings: Not of value in psychotic patients. Caution against hazardous occupations requiring complete mental alertness. When used adjunctively in convulsive disorders, possibility of increase in frequency and/or severity of grand mal seizures may require increased dosage of standard anticonvulsant medication; abrupt withdrawal may be associated with temporary increase in frequency and/or severity of seizures. Advise against simultaneous ingestion of alcohol and other CNS depressants. Withdrawal symptoms have occurred following abrupt discontinuance. Keep addiction-prone individuals under careful surveillance because of their predisposition to habituation and dependence. In pregnancy, lactation or women of childbearing age, weigh potential benefit against possible hazard.

Precautions: If combined with other psychotropics or anticonvulsants, consider carefully pharmacology of agents employed. Usual precautions indicated in patients severely depressed, or with latent depression, or with suicidal tendencies. Observe usual precautions in impaired renal or hepatic function. Limit dosage to smallest effective amount in elderly and debilitated to preclude ataxia or oversedation.

Side Effects: Drowsiness, confusion, diplopia, hypotension, changes in libido, nausea, fatigue, depression, dysarthria, jaundice, skin rash, ataxia, constipation, headache, incontinence, changes in salivation, slurred speech, tremor, vertigo, urinary retention, blurred vision. Paradoxical reactions such as acute hyperexcited states, anxiety, hallucinations, increased muscle spasticity, insomnia, rage, sleep disturbances, stimulation, have been reported; should these occur, discontinue drug. Isolated reports of neutropenia, jaundice; periodic blood counts and liver function tests advisable during long-term therapy.

Valium® (diazepam)

2-mg, 5-mg, 10-mg tablets

to help relieve psychic tension and its somatic symptoms

[From Medical World News, January 8, 1971]

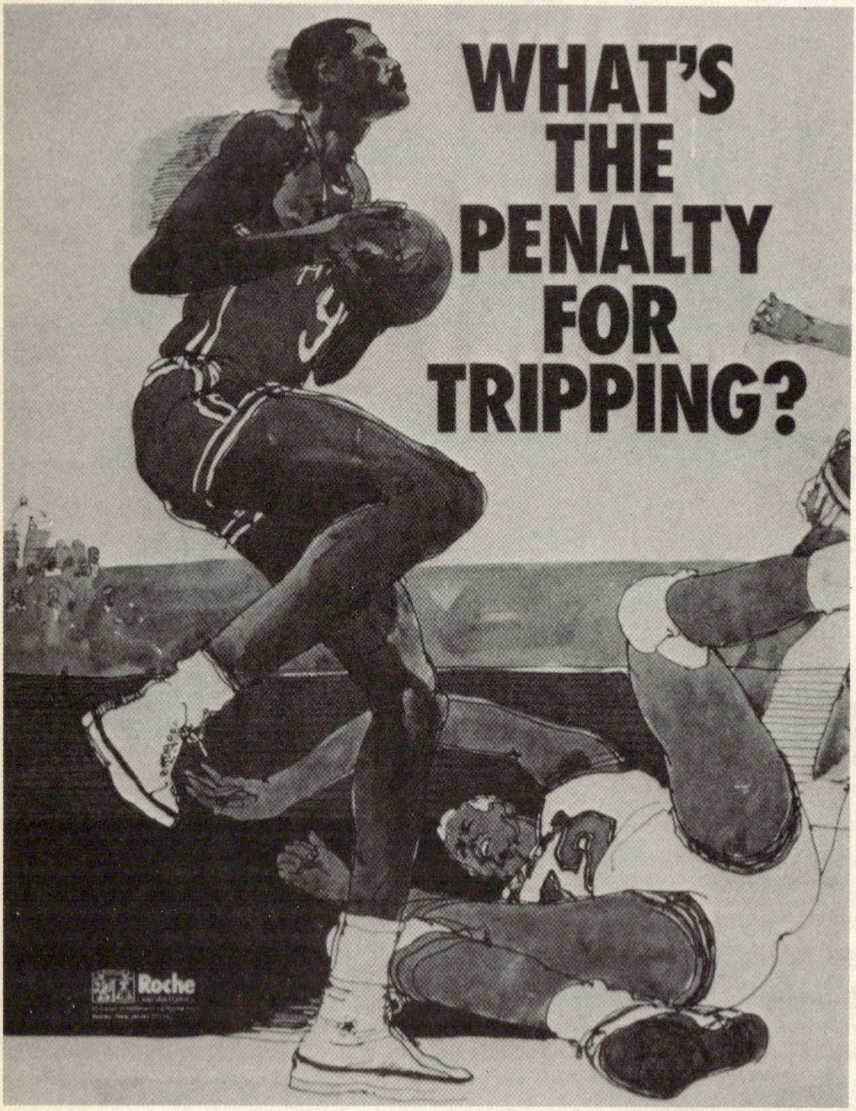

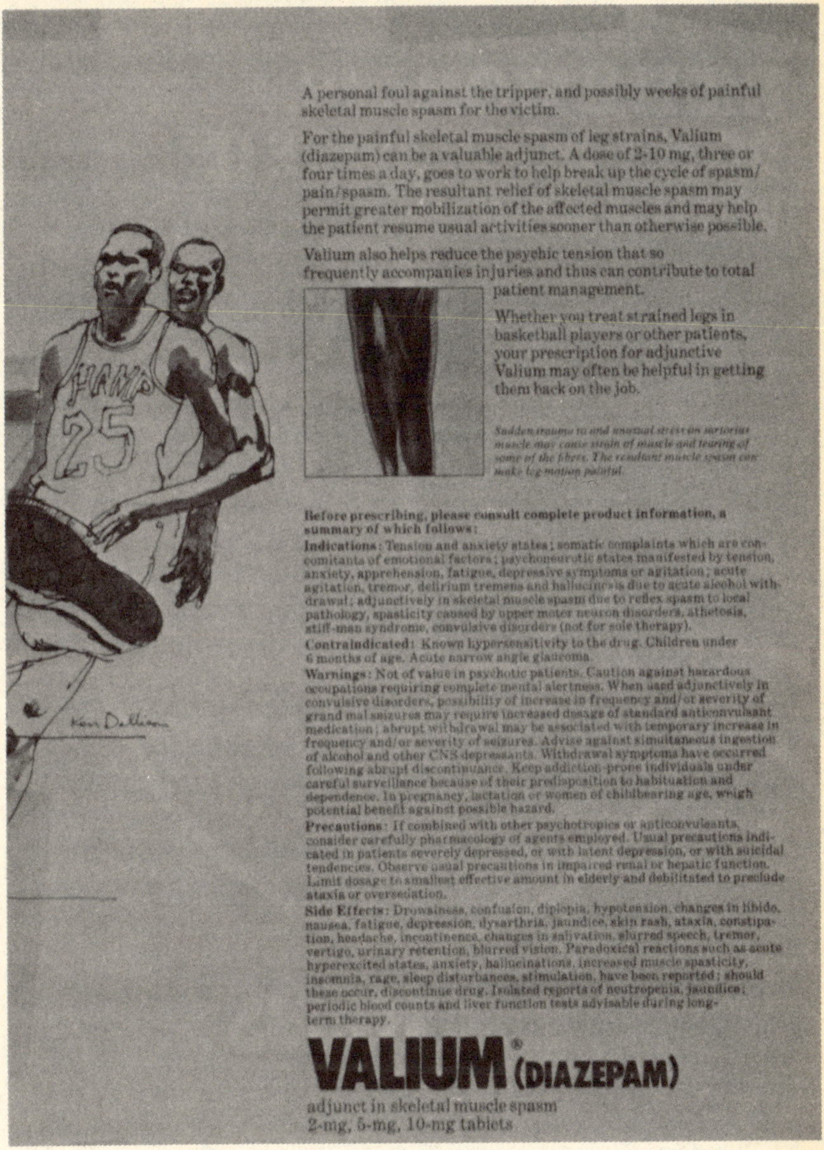
A personal foul against the tripper, and possibly weeks of painful skeletal muscle spasm for the victim.
For the painful skeletal muscle spasm of leg strains, Valium (diazepam) can be a valuable adjunct. A dose of 2-10 mg, three or four times a day, goes to work to help break up the cycle of spasm/pain/spasm. The resultant relief of skeletal muscle spasm may permit greater mobilization of the affected muscles and may help the patient resume usual activities sooner than otherwise possible.
Valium also helps reduce the psychic tension that so frequently accompanies injuries and thus can contribute to total patient management.
Whether you treat strained legs in basketball players or other patients, your prescription for adjunctive Valium may often be helpful in getting them back on the job.
Sudden trauma to and unusual stress on sartorius muscle may cause strain of muscle and tearing of some of the fibres. The resultant muscle spasm can make leg motion painful.
Before prescribing, please consult complete product information, a summary of which follows:
Indications: Tension and anxiety states; somatic complaints which are concomitants of emotional factors; psychoneurotic states manifested by tension, anxiety, apprehension, fatigue, depressive symptoms or agitation; acute agitation, tremor, delirium tremens and hallucinosis due to acute alcohol withdrawal; adjunctively in skeletal muscle spasm due to reflex spasm to local pathology, spasticity caused by upper motor neuron disorders, athetosis, stiff-man syndrome, convulsive disorders (not for sole therapy).
Contraindicated: Known hypersensitivity to the drug. Children under 6 months of age. Acute narrow angle glaucoma.
Warnings: Not of value in psychotic patients. Caution against hazardous occupations requiring complete mental alertness. When used adjunctively in convulsive disorders, possibility of increase in frequency and/or severity of grand mal seizures may require increased dosage of standard anticonvulsant medication; abrupt withdrawal may be associated with temporary increase in frequency and/or severity of seizures. Advise against simultaneous ingestion of alcohol and other CNS depressants. Withdrawal symptoms have occurred following abrupt discontinuance. Keep addiction-prone individuals under careful surveillance because of their predisposition to habituation and dependence. In pregnancy, lactation or women of childbearing age, weigh potential benefit against possible hazard.
Precautions: If combined with other psychotropics or anticonvulsants, consider carefully pharmacology of agents employed. Usual precautions indicated in patients severely depressed, or with latent depression, or with suicidal tendencies. Observe usual precautions in impaired renal or hepatic function. Limit dosage to smallest effective amount in elderly and debilitated to preclude ataxia or oversedation.
Side Effects: Drowsiness, confusion, diplopia, hypotension, changes in libido, nausea, fatigue, depression, dysarthria, jaundice, skin rash, ataxia, constipation, headache, incontinence, changes in salivation, slurred speech, tremor, vertigo, urinary retention, blurred vision. Paradoxical reactions such as acute hyperexcited states, anxiety, hallucinations, increased muscle spasticity, insomnia, rage, sleep disturbances, stimulation, have been reported; should these occur, discontinue drug. Isolated reports of neutropenia, jaundice; periodic blood counts and liver function tests advisable during long-term therapy.
VALIUM® (DIAZEPAM)
adjunct in skeletal muscle spasm
2-mg, 5-mg, 10-mg tablets

normal activities of life. Medical-journal advertising, reproduced on these pages, suggested apprehension about "unstable national and world conditions,"[10] "exposure to new friends,"[11] "raising a young family,"[12] writing a doctoral dissertation[13] and being a mother with "too little time" to pursue a "vocation for which she has spent many years in training"[14] as proper occasions for prescribing a tranquilizer. Many advertisements that promoted Valium and its cousins for "tension and anxiety" depicted women; other advertisements, which promoted Valium as an adjunct in treating muscle spasm, depicted male athletes.[15]

During the 1970s, unfavorable attention was directed at the disproportionate use of tranquilizers by women. The spotlight of disapproval focused on advertising that encouraged physicians to regard women's legitimate complaints as proper occasions for drugging them.

Several women's groups, as well as health and consumer organizations, addressed this problem. In 1979, the House Select Committee on Narcotics Abuse and Control held hearings that probed the use of psychoactive drugs among women.

By the end of the 1970s, Roche, the manufacturer of Valium, along with other manufacturers of tranquilizers, had shifted their advertising focus to fields that appeared to be less susceptible to public outcry. New advertisements taught physicians to view the stresses of mature life as indications for the use of Valium.

Doctors were also encouraged to use Valium as an "adjunct" to the treatment of various physical conditions, both organic (having a definite physical cause) and functional (not directly related to a known disease). The lay person would be poorly equipped to question such a prescription; the physician would feel that if he failed to prescribe Valium to his physically ill patient, he was somehow remiss for not treating the "whole" disease.

During the late 1970s, Roche mailed physicians a series of brochures entitled "Psychosocial Forces in Primary Medicine."[16] This series included topics such as Job Change, Separation, Divorce and Couple Breakup, Midlife, and Aging.

Carefully written, tastefully illustrated, and copiously documented from scientific sources, these brochures themselves refrained from pushing any specific drug. Tucked inside each envelope, however, was a flyer advertising Valium.[17]

This flyer could easily leave the reader with the unmistakable impression that Valium is the answer to the normal stresses of life, rather than a powerful drug to be reserved for severe anxiety states.

Each stage of life presents its special stresses; this is perfectly normal and consistent with our understanding of people as constantly growing, developing beings. Stress is part of change, and coping with stress is something each person can and must master. Stress as an abnormal condition to be treated with a pill has been, for the most part, a creation of the drug industry, which promotes sales by convincing doctors that patients coping with difficult life situations must take medicine to dull their response to those circumstances.

The pushers of Valium and its cousins have regarded every developmental stage of life—indeed, daily life itself—as an occasion to take a drug, even, as we shall see, when such drugs might be particularly dangerous.

Although Valium and its cousins hold special dangers for older people (as described in Chapter 3), this has not deterred Roche from concentrating much of its recent advertising on the promotion of Valium for use among the elderly.

In 1979, Roche sent brochures to physicians encouraging the use of Valium for older people. One, entitled,

"The later years . . . An optimistic outlook," described Valium as "an important component of treatment programs for relief of excessive geriatric [old age] anxiety and psychic tension."[18]

Another brochure from Roche, entitled, "Stress and the Senior Citizen: A Time for Reappraisal," contained no specific reference to Valium, although it mentioned pharmacologic therapy. However, tucked inside each mailing envelope was a flyer entitled "Talking over Valium (diazepam) Therapy with your Patient."[19]

Early in the 1980s, Roche sent physicians a series of handsomely illustrated brochures entitled, "Roche Seminars on Aging." As in the Psychosocial Forces series, Roche refrained from touting Valium in the tastefully prepared text, confining Valium literature to a "centerfold" section. Here, Valium was recommended as appropriate for the elderly with "limited" coping skills, facing "not only the constraints brought about by their own reduced capabilitites, *but also those imposed by the social structure and environment*" (emphasis added).[20]

As earlier advertising had recommended Valium and its cousins for students, women, and people in mid-life facing difficult adjustments to external difficulties, these advertisements once again instructed physicians that the proper response to the plight of the individual limited by the "social structure" or "environment" is a psychoactive drug—presumably so the patient would be tranquilized into accepting these limitations—notwithstanding the special risks of the benzodiazepines for the elderly.

Advertisements promoting Valium and its cousins for the normal stresses of life reached a crescendo in the late 1970s—in spite of warnings from the U.S. Food and Drug Administration as early as 1971. On October 22, 1971,

FDA commissioner Charles C. Edwards wrote to drug companies, saying:

> Of late, advertisements have also promoted [these drugs'] use in the treatment of symptoms arising from the stresses of everyday living, which cannot properly be defined as pathological. . . . [Drug companies are] requested to promptly cancel all advertising and promotion of such drugs which recommend or suggest their use for everyday or minor life stresses. . . .[21]

In 1980, the FDA finally stepped in to stop this line of advertising. From then on, the required product labeling setting forth the indications for the use of the drug was to include the following statement:

> [Name of anxiolytic] is indicated for the management of anxiety disorders or for the short term relief of the symptoms of anxiety. Anxiety or tension associated with the stress of everyday life usually does not require treatment with an anxiolytic [a drug intended for the relief of anxiety].[22]

Anticipation of this directive was the cue for drug manufacturers to strike out, like Marco Polos of advertising, to discover and develop new "markets" where none had existed before. Today, simple anxiety and muscle spasm are no longer the only reasons given by drug companies for prescribing a tranquilizer such as Valium. Rather, physicians are implicitly encouraged to view almost every human ill as an occasion for such a prescription.

Medical advances are extending the physically healthy years

An ever-increasing number of people are enjoying longer and healthier lives as a result of medical advances and improved health care. Many diseases once considered incurable can now be managed. Medical and surgical innovations, effective medications and improved nutrition have not only increased longevity but have improved the quality of life. As a consequence, today's older generation is "young-old" rather than "old-old;" the majority remain vigorous even into the seventies.[1]

The elderly now represent 11% of the population—there are more than 22,000,000 persons over 65—and their numbers continue to grow.[2] Biological and medical sciences are steadily expanding gerontological research, minimizing morbidity and increasing life expectancy.[3] The National Institute on Aging (NIH) is but one of the growing number of agencies pursuing promising leads on the retardation of physical decline and the management of degenerative diseases that victimize the elderly more than people in other age groups.

Psychiatric, social and psychological advances are improving emotional well-being

Increased longevity can frequently lead to increased anxiety in the lives of many of our aging. Bereavement, of course, is a major stress But even in those who are fortunate enough not to suffer it, there are other sources of anxiety. Retirement, for example, brings on problems that are often psychological as well as financial.[4] For a large number of the elderly, th aim of modern therapy is to try to maintain psychological as well as physical intactness. I addition to psychotherapy, frequently of valu there are now many resources for the elderly help them cope with their problems and enri their lives.

Social agencies, community centers, religious organizations and senior citizen group are providing recreational, cultural and educa tional activities to help satisfy the need for po itive social experiences. The homebound sen citizen also has a number of services availabl to him—Homemaker Home-Health Aide personnel, The Visiting Nurse Association, Meal on-Wheels and various volunteer telephone services to provide daily contact.[5]

By raising the age for mandatory retirement from 65 to 70, the Government is encouraging senior citizens to continue work ing. Ultimately, it may experiment with flexib work schedules suited to the elderly; it may a inaugurate retraining programs to enable th to work at less strenuous—or more interesting—jobs.[6] More and more, universiti are promoting the idea of second careers for older people by offering "late start" education opportunities.

The elderly themselves are launching the own self-help programs. They are learning th they can exercise considerable power and are working through such groups as the Gray Panthers to achieve their goals.

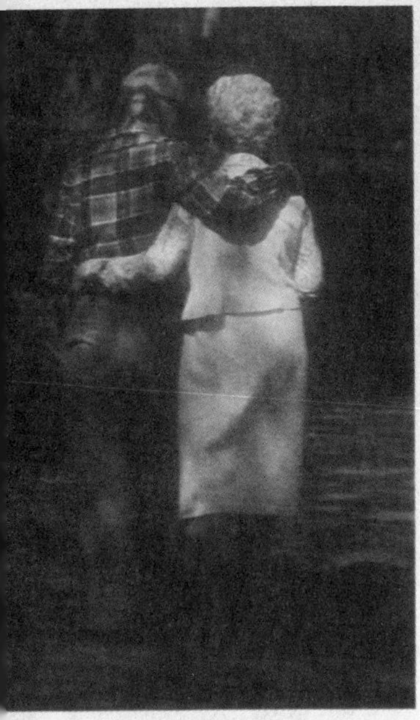

ven in patients with notional problems, there's ·ason for optimism

general, stresses are more taxing when ·ople grow older. Loss of a loved one, the fam- home, or a career engenders anxiety at a ne when the individual is physically and notionally least able to adapt and to cope.[7] hat is remarkable, however, is the strength splayed by so many of the elderly in dealing ith these stresses.

With the help of the physician, many of the ressors affecting the elderly can be alleviated. ome people, in involuntary retirement, can be ncouraged to find a meaningful and reward- g substitute occupation. Others can be uided into making constructive decisions re- ırding changes in their lives, thereby replac- g practical, rational approaches for emotional ıes.[4] And the supportive care, friendly per- ıasion and empathy of the primary care ıysician are of inestimable value in enhanc- g physical and emotional well-being in the ıxious elderly patient.[8]

ferences: 1. Greater longevity said to bring longer stresses. *Psychiatr ws 13* (10): 38-39, May 19, 1978. **2.** Medical News: *JAMA 240*:1325- 26, Sept 22, 1978. **3.** Mooney CM: *J Am Geriatr Soc 26*:268-273, June '8. **4.** Merrill GG: *Med Times 106*:10d-16d, Jan 1978. **5.** Blazer D: *iatrics 33*:117-123, Feb 1978. **6.** Carlson E: *Mod Maturity 21*:15-16, -Jan 1978-79. **7.** Fann WE, Wheless JC: The recognition and man- ement of anxiety in geriatric patients in nursing homes. Presented at cerpta Medica symposium, Clinical Anxiety/Tension in Primary Medi- e, Washington, DC, Sept 1977. **8.** Mead BT: *Geriatrics 32*:73-77, Oct 77.

efore prescribing, please see complete oduct information under flap.

If pharmacological support is indicated, Valium® (diazepam/Roche) 2 mg is especially appropriate

Judicious use of a minor tranquilizer can be an important component of treatment programs for relief of excessive geriatric anxiety and psychic tension. Because of its special advantages and low-dose effectiveness, Valium is an excellent choice. Many of the elderly patient's anxiety-related somatic symptoms, such as headache, gastrointestinal distress, fatigue and insomnia, respond as well.[7] Also, Valium can be used with most primary medications, including cardiac glycosides, vasodilators, diuretics and anticoagulants. And since older patients are often subject to skeletal muscle spasm related to inflammation of muscles or joints, they can also benefit from the muscle-relaxant properties of adjunctive Valium.

Fortunately, side effects are relatively infrequent and seldom severe. Drowsiness, fatigue and ataxia may occur but can usually be avoided by using the smallest effective dosage. The 2-mg strength is designed to mitigate such occurrences or minimize oversedation. As with all CNS-acting agents, patients should be cautioned against driving, operating dangerous machinery or ingesting alcohol while taking Valium. Periodic reassessment of the need for a psychotropic agent is also recommended.

When the emotional problem is excessive anxiety and tension

VALIUM® (IV)

diazepam/Roche

2-mg scored tablets

STRESS AND THE SENIOR CITIZEN

A time for reappraisal

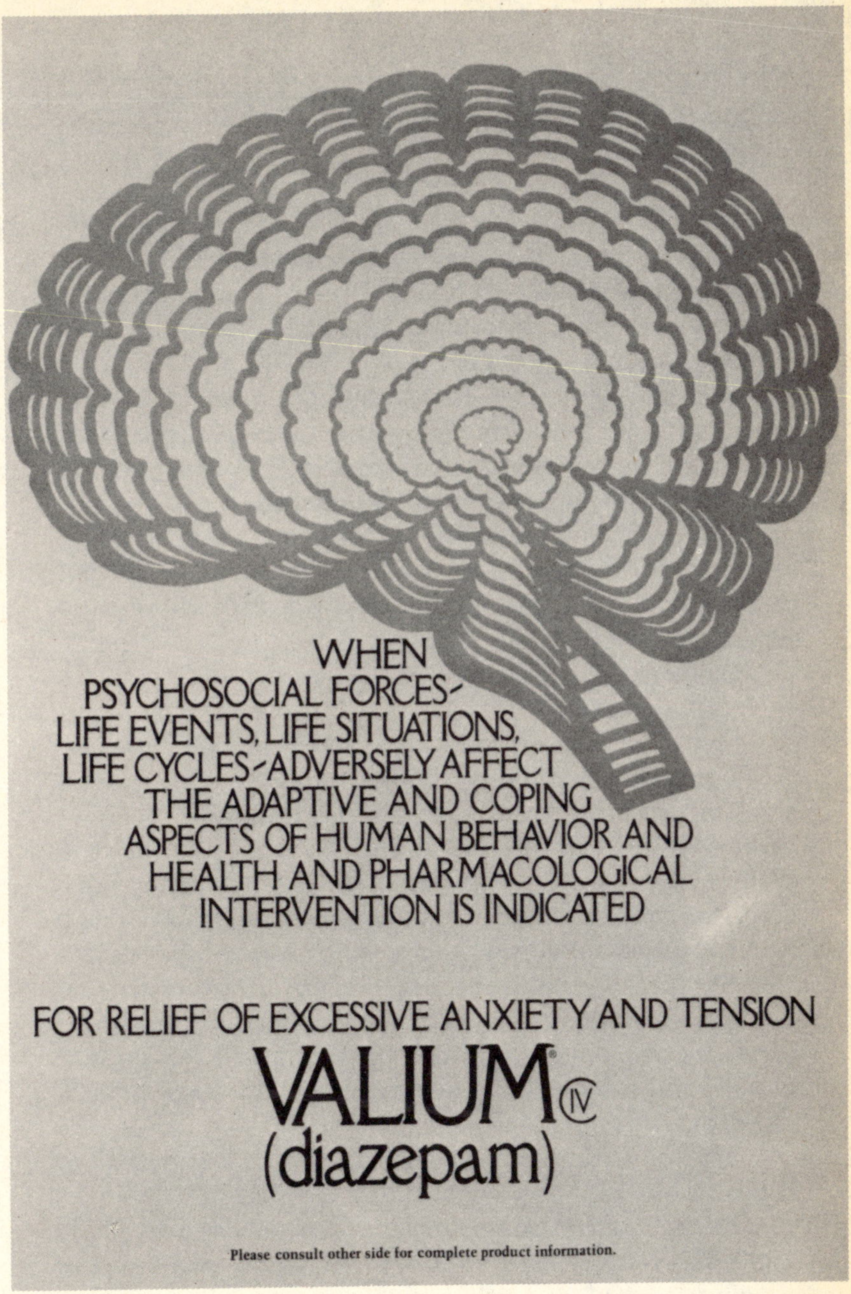
WHEN
PSYCHOSOCIAL FORCES-
LIFE EVENTS, LIFE SITUATIONS,
LIFE CYCLES-ADVERSELY AFFECT
THE ADAPTIVE AND COPING
ASPECTS OF HUMAN BEHAVIOR AND
HEALTH AND PHARMACOLOGICAL
INTERVENTION IS INDICATED
FOR RELIEF OF EXCESSIVE ANXIETY AND TENSION
VALIUM® (IV)
(diazepam)
Please consult other side for complete product information.

Drug Advertising Today

Colorful brochures sent to physicians, as well as page after page of journal advertising, present a seemingly limitless series of ills and non-ills for which Valium might be prescribed.

Non-ills? Certainly! The parade of non-ills for which physicians have been implicitly encouraged to prescribe Valium and its cousins has had different marchers over the years, but the beat has remained the same.

A decade ago, the simple fact of being a woman going to college for the first time, or trapped at home with small children and half a dozen mops, was evidence of the need for Valium or one of its relations. Later, coping with midlife problems or aging was offered as a justification for such treatment.

Most recently, doctors have received mailings suggesting a more ingenious use of a nondisease as an occasion for drug use. In this campaign, headlined "Negative Tests—Positive Symptoms," Valium is suggested for individuals experiencing symptoms of illness such as heart disease—symptoms presumed to be caused by anxiety—with no test results suggesting the actual presence of such disease.[23] The advertisement suggests first starting the patient on Valium and then providing reassurance about his physical complaint, rather than providing that reassurance initially and helping the patient deal with his anxiety without drugs.

The unwritten message to doctors is clear: patient complaining of "heart symptoms"? Give Valium!

Roche's advertising for the mid-1970s and early 1980s has also stressed the use of Valium as an adjunct in treating other physical illnesses.[24,25]

The use of an anti-anxiety drug—especially for short-term use in certain acutely ill patients, such as heart-attack victims—is sometimes appropriate. However, advertising that promotes the use of Valium or any benzodiazepine for the anxiety said to accompany high blood pressure and gastrointestinal disorders (such as ulcers), or the use of Valium in connection with cardiac surgery, tends to give the impression that many such patients will suffer from such unmanageable anxiety that a drug will be needed to control it. Such a message may create anxiety in the physician, who may feel that if he or she does not automatically prescribe such a drug along with other medication for the physical condition, he or she is somehow practicing bad medicine.

Sometimes the advertising, the labeling, and the actual characteristics of the various members of the benzodiazepine family do not coincide.

It is well known for instance, that Valium and Librium, like all benzodiazepines, can cause drowsiness. This is one of the most common side effects mentioned in the drug labeling for these products, and patients are cautioned about driving or engaging in other tasks requiring mental alertness. Yet neither Valium nor Librium is advertised or approved as a sleeping pill.

Dalmane, on the other hand, has been so approved by the FDA and is marketed for this purpose.

A few years ago, Roche found these three top-selling products in a position to compete with each other, a situation that Roche definitely wished to avoid.

In 1977, the National Institute of Drug Abuse prepared a booklet on sleeping pills entitled "Sedative-Hypnotic Drugs, Risks and Benefits."[26] This booklet mentioned Valium and Librium, as well as Dalmane, as having sedative-hypnotic [sleep-inducing] effects, although the two former drugs had never been approved as sleeping pills by the FDA.

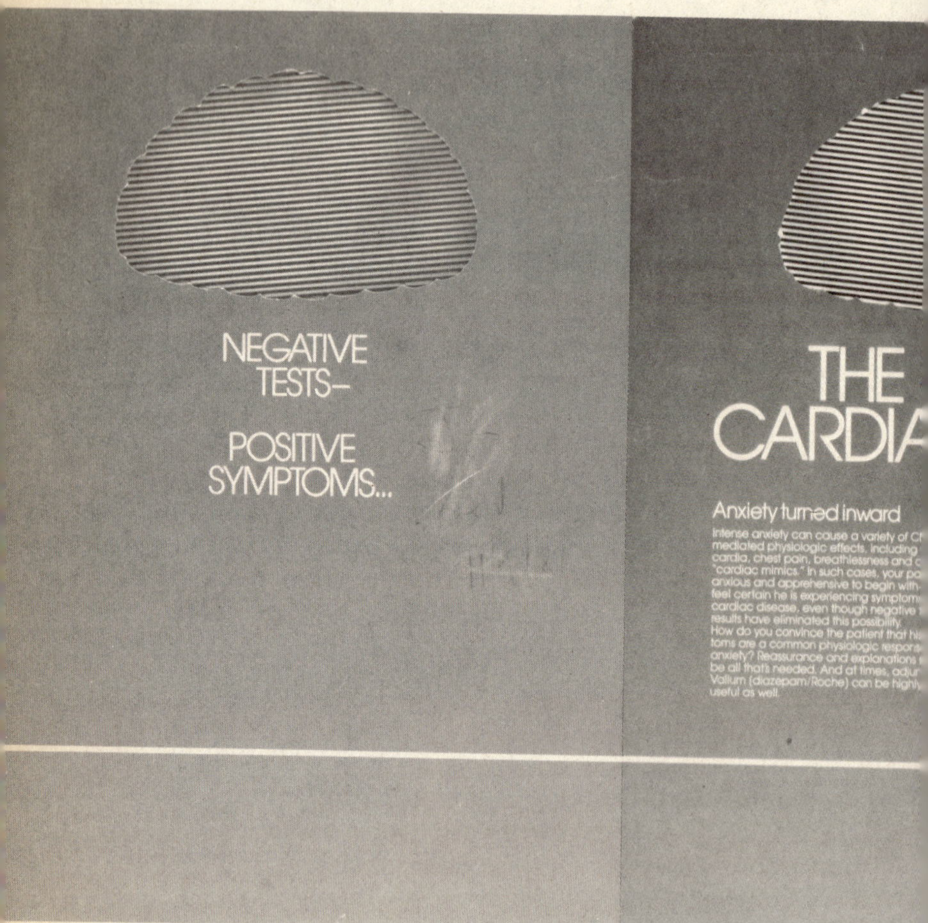
NEGATIVE TESTS–
POSITIVE SYMPTOMS...
THE
CARDIA
Anxiety turned inward
Intense anxiety can cause a variety of
mediated physiologic effects, including
cardia, chest pain, breathlessness and
"cardiac mimics." In such cases, your
anxious and apprehensive to begin with
feel certain he is experiencing
cardiac disease, even though negative
results have eliminated this possibility.
How do you convince the patient that
toms are a common physiologic
anxiety? Reassurance and explanations
be all that's needed. And at times,
Valium (diazepam/Roche) can be
useful as well.

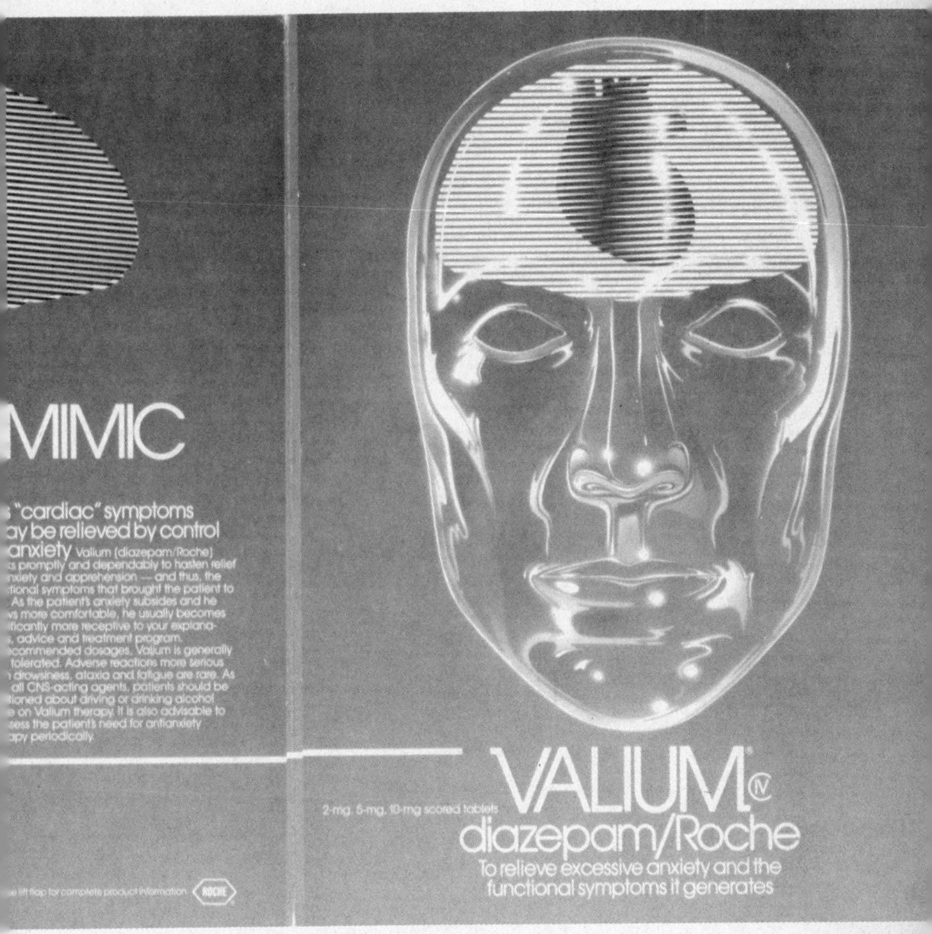
MIMIC
s "cardiac" symptoms
ay be relieved by control
anxiety Valium (diazepam/Roche)
s promptly and dependably to hasten relief
nxiety and apprehension — and thus, the
tional symptoms that brought the patient to
As the patient's anxiety subsides and he
s more comfortable, he usually becomes
ficantly more receptive to your explana-
, advice and treatment program.
ecommended dosages, Valium is generally
tolerated. Adverse reactions more serious
drowsiness, ataxia and fatigue are rare. As
all CNS-acting agents, patients should be
tioned about driving or drinking alcohol
e on Valium therapy. It is also advisable to
sess the patient's need for antianxiety
apy periodically.
e lift flap for complete product information
ROCHE
2-mg, 5-mg, 10-mg scored tablets
VALIUM® ⓘⓥ
diazepam/Roche
To relieve excessive anxiety and the
functional symptoms it generates

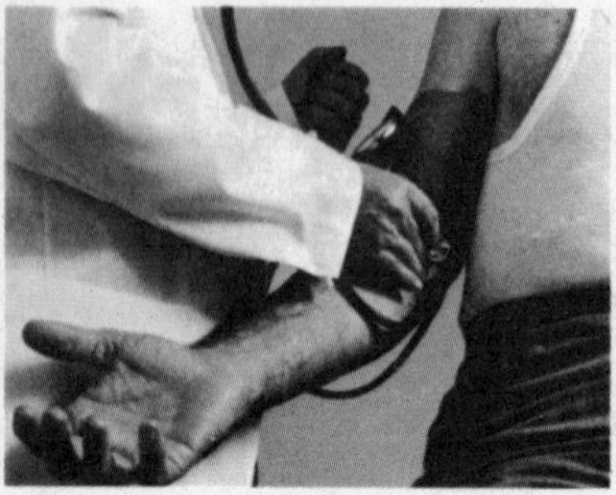

Do you also take a reading of the hypertensive patient's psychic tension?

Here's how and why Valium® (diazepam) can be useful as an adjunct

In certain patients, aggravation of an existing hypertensive state by emotional stress can become a problem. Therefore, management of this type of hypertensive patient often includes control of psychic tension. Your initial treatment methods may consist of counseling, reassurance and relaxation techniques. But if the patient fails to respond adequately to these measures, Valium (diazepam) can be an excellent choice for adjunctive therapy.

Most anxious hypertensive patients experience relief of their anxiety-related symptoms within the first few days of therapy with Valium. In choosing Valium it is also important that Valium is used with most classes of primary medications such as cardiac glycosides, diuretics, vasodilators, anticoagulants, anticholinergics, antacids and antihypertensives. However, due care should be given to the pharmacology of the agents to be combined, particularly compounds that may potentiate the action of Valium (diazepam).

In addition, an *h.s.* dose of Valium added to a *b.i.d.* or *t.i.d.* regimen can bring relief if psychic tension symptoms are pronounced at bedtime.

In recommended dosage, oral Valium (diazepam) rarely produces significant side effects. As with most CNS-acting agents, patients should be cautioned against driving or operating dangerous machinery.

When anxiety and tension complicate the management of the hypertensive patient, consider adjunctive Valium for its psychotherapeutic effect.

adjunct for the overly tense hypertensive patient

Valium® (diazepam)

2-mg, 5-mg, 10-mg tablets ROCHE

Please lift flap for complete product information.

THE PATIENT'S "PSYCHOSOCIAL PROFILE" ADDS VALUABLE INSIGHTS...

Assessment often includes, as well, the patient's emotional status. Researchers have found that psychological and social factors may play a role in the development of hypertension. (They've found, for instance, that plasma renin activity in humans appears to increase with experimental stress.)[5] The subject is both complex and controversial. Less controversial, though, is the recommendation often made that some form of "psychosocial profile" be added to the patient's family and medical history.[2,6]

In essence, this acknowledges the fact that an understanding of the patient's current social, economic and psychologic status can be valuable. Perhaps the patient's hypertension has been aggravated recently by a major life event—a family upheaval, or an occupational setback. If so, the physician will want to know about it. He will also want to assess the patient's understanding of his illness, his emotional reaction to it—and his potential for complying with the recommended therapeutic program. Information such as this can help set the stage for the kind of mutually rewarding doctor-patient relationship that is often essential to successful long-term management of any chronic illness.

References:
1. Med World News 20(13):34-44, June 25, 1979
2. Caldwell JR: Postgrad Med 65:66-77, May 1979
3. Rakel RE et al: Primary Cardiol 5:102-109, Sept 1979
4. Lucas CP, Omar M: Geriatrics 35:51-59, Jan 1980
5. Clamage DM, Vander AJ, Mouw DR: Psychosom Med 39(6):393, 1977
6. Perloff D: Geriatrics 31:77-83, Jan 1976

...AND OFTEN IT REVEALS EXCESSIVE ANXIETY

Although the hypertensive patient may seem calm enough on the surface, a few carefully worded questions may uncover intense anxiety symptoms. The patient's anxiety may center on his physical problems alone, or may extend as well to the economic and social repercussions of his illness. In addition, he may be having difficulty coping with the medical "do's and don'ts" he now faces—and with his demoralizing new self-image as a "chronically sick, potentially dependent" person.

In many cases, your reassurance and continued support will be enough to relieve the emotional distress. But for some patients, you may find that specific antianxiety medication is also warranted. And it is at these times that Valium (diazepam/Roche) can be especially helpful. Valium works promptly—predictably—to relieve the excessive anxiety that so often accompanies organic illness. Initial calming typically occurs within hours—more sustained and definitive symptomatic relief of anxiety in a matter of days. With his intense anxiety under control, the hypertensive patient is generally better able to face his condition and to comply with your treatment program.

Equally important, Valium is used with most classes of primary medications, such as cardiac glycosides, diuretics, vasodilators and other antihypertensives. Valium is usually well tolerated. Side effects more serious than drowsiness, fatigue and ataxia are rare. As with all CNS-acting agents, patients should be cautioned against drinking alcoholic beverages or driving while on Valium therapy. Periodic assessment of the continued need for psychotropic agents is recommended and, once the patient is again able to cope, Valium should be gradually discontinued.

VALIUM® (IV)

diazepam/Roche

2-mg, 5-mg, 10-mg scored tablets

WHEN EXCESSIVE ANXIETY HAMPERS THE ABILITY TO COPE

Valium (diazepam) **adjunctively**

If your ulcer patient's psychic tension and anxiety continue to remain at high levels, you may find it useful to add Valium to his regimen. Valium works promptly: in a few days, the patient should feel significantly calmer and less anxious. Valium is used with most classes of primary medications such as antacids and anticholinergics.

When psychic tension and anxiety are particularly pronounced at bedtime—as is often the case with ulcer patients—the addition of an h.s. dose of Valium to a b.i.d. or t.i.d. regimen can reduce these symptoms and thus may encourage sleep.

Oral Valium is usually well tolerated. In the elderly and debilitated patient, initial therapy should be limited to the smallest effective dose (2 to 2½ mg once or twice daily) to preclude development of ataxia or oversedation. Once symptoms have been reduced to tolerable levels, therapy should be discontinued.

Valium® (diazepam) Ⓒ IV
2-mg, 5-mg, 10-mg scored tablets
can relieve the ulcer patient's excessive anxiety

Before prescribing, please consult complete product information on following pages.

X-ray of a typical "active-stage" duodenal ulcer

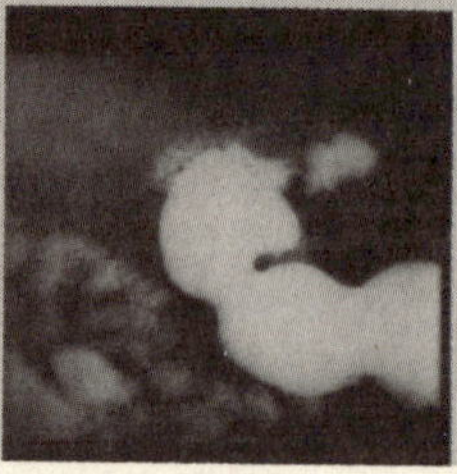

Roche wished to give copies of these booklets to physicians, primarily as a promotional device for Dalmane, its sleeping pill. The FDA expressed concern that Roche's distribution of the booklet would give the impression that Librium and Valium had been approved as sleeping pills, and so Roche drew up a careful plan of presentation to avoid any suggestion that this was the case.

At a meeting held in 1979 on this topic, a lawyer for Roche offered assurances that the book would only be distributed by detailmen making a sales pitch to doctors for Dalmane (flurazepam), Roche's benzodiazepine sleeping pill. He said that Roche had

> no intention to use the book in any way for Valium or Librium—[that] it would not be in the best interests of the company to do so, since if what . . . [the FDA] said was true, it would "cut into" Dalmane sales and emphasize effects of Valium and Librium they do not want to emphasize.

The Roche lawyer explained that his company did *"not want Valium and Librium to be thought of as a sedative since they promote the drugs as daytime tranquilizers"* (emphasis added).[27]

As we have seen, there are no substantial differences in the ability of the various members of the benzodiazepine family to promote sleep or alleviate anxiety. Nevertheless, Roche has carefully carved out different market areas for products that are essentially the same in these respects.

Earlier, Roche had suggested that Valium was the drug to prescribe for ulcer patients "when psychic tension and anxiety are particularly pronounced at bedtime" because the drug could "reduce these symptoms and thus may encourage sleep."[28]

IN THE ANXIOUS POST-MI PATIENT

THESE PARAMETERS MAY BE IMPROVING...

The patient's ECG shows an improved picture with virtually no signs of the S-T segment shift associated with myocardial injury. Both the erythrocyte sedimentation rate and the SGOT are now within normal limits. Blood pressure readings are on the low side and the patient's pulse rate is down to 80 beats per minute. The atrial gallop sound can no longer be heard.

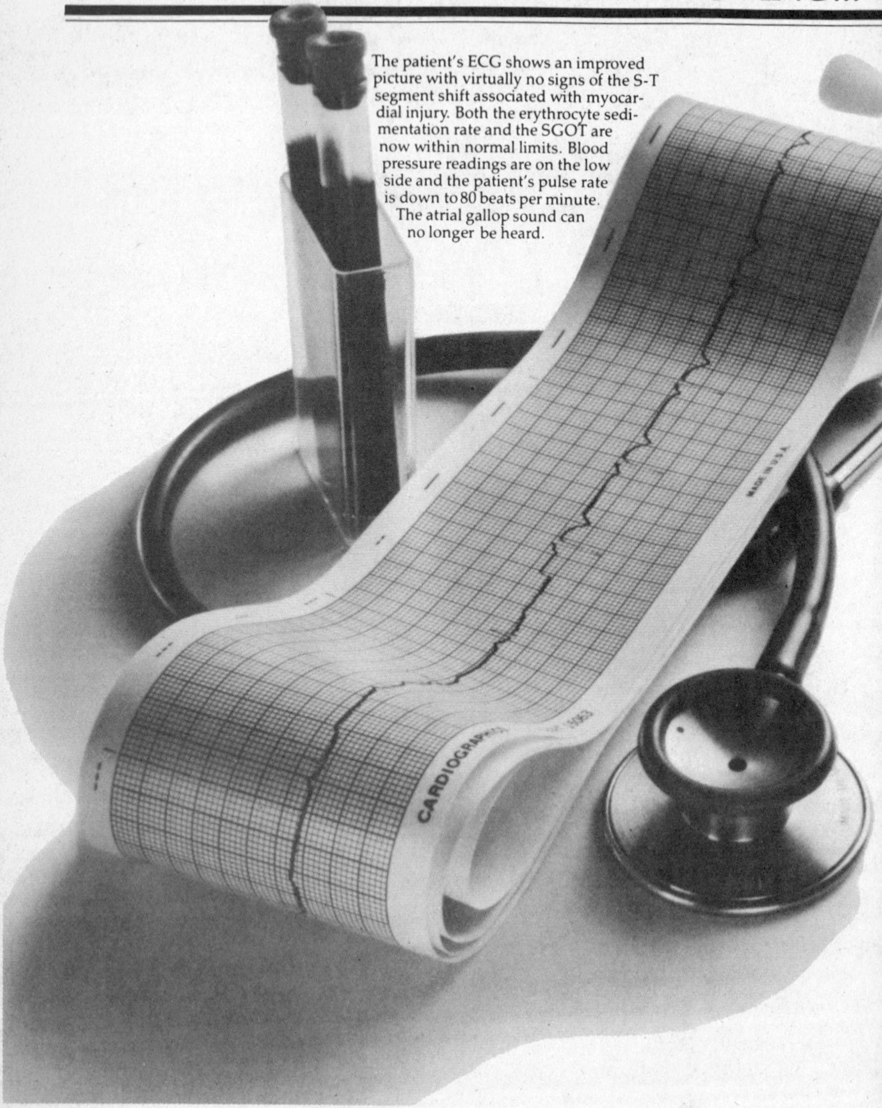

BUT THESE MAY NOT

You've assured the patient, time and again, that he's making excellent progress, that all signs point to a marked improvement in his condition. He *seems* to understand... and yet, his excessive anxiety and psychic tension continue to pose problems.

For patients like this, adjunctive Valium (diazepam) can be particularly useful. Valium works promptly: patients often feel distinctly calmer in hours, usually report significant symptomatic relief within days. And once calmer and in better control of their emotions, they tend to be more optimistic as well and to enter more willingly into rehabilitative programs.

Valium can also alleviate the anxiety-linked insomnia so often seen in post-MI patients. In most cases, adding an *h.s.* dose of Valium to the usual *t.i.d.* schedule helps relieve "nighttime apprehensions" and encourages sleep. And Valium is used with most classes of primary medications, including cardiac glycosides, anticoagulants, diuretics and vasodilators.

An especially important advantage: Valium is usually well tolerated. Though drowsiness, ataxia and fatigue are encountered with some patients, these and more serious side effects are rarely a problem. Patients who will be taking Valium during their first weeks at home should be cautioned against the simultaneous drinking of alcohol. Periodic reassessment of the patient's need for psychotropic medication is also recommended.

feelings of tension
difficulty in falling asleep
loss of interest
inability to relax

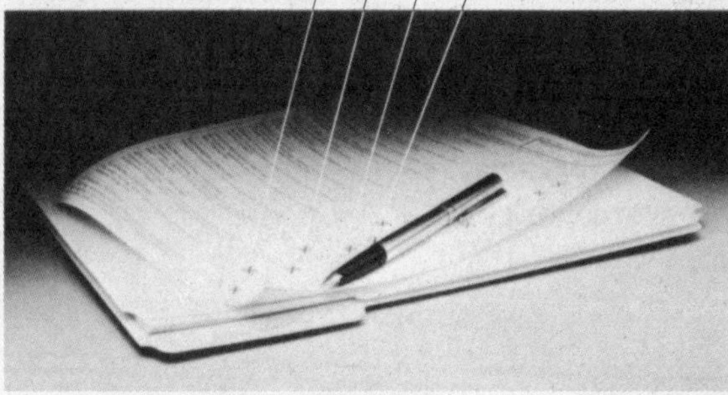

VALIUM® Ⓘⓥ
diazepam/Roche

2-mg, 5-mg, 10-mg scored tablets

TO HELP STABILIZE
THE PATIENT'S ANXIETY

Before prescribing, please see complete product information under fold. ROCHE

And in 1979, "difficulty in falling asleep" was one of the symptoms by which a physician could identify anxiety calling for the use of Valium in a recovering heart attack patient:

> Valium can also alleviate the anxiety-linked insomnia so often seen in post-[heart attack] patients. In most cases, adding a [bedtime] dose of Valium to the usual [three times a day] schedule helps relieve "night-time apprehensions" and *encourages sleep* (emphasis added).[29]

Thus, Roche managed to avoid competition between its own products, continued to promote a sedating drug for daytime use, and yet subtly conveyed a message to doctors about the nighttime use of its products, all within the framework of FDA control of advertising claims.

Drug Advertising: Fact or Fiction?

Not only has Valium's manufacturer implicitly encouraged physicians to prescribe drugs for non-illnesses or as adjuncts for treatment of physical illnesses where they might not be necessary, but it has also published downright inaccurate information in advertising for physicians.

At least twice during 1981 and 1982, the Public Citizen Health Research Group was instrumental in causing the "recall" of false and misleading advertising for Valium.

During 1981, a rather atypical series of advertisements for Valium began to appear in medical journals. Produced in plain black and white, in contrast to the bright colors of Roche's customary Valium advertising, these advertisements featured Valium speaking in the first person in its own behalf. *Examine Me,* said the "Talking Pill" in one of these advertisements; *Think About This,* suggest the Pill in yet another. In a third advertisement, headlined "Feelings vs. Facts," the Talking Pill again urged physicians to disregard mounting evidence of the dangers of Valium.

While in each of these advertisements, the Talking Pill reassured the physician of its safety, in one, "Feelings vs. Facts," the Pill went so far as to state, "I do not cause physical dependence if the recommended dosages and therapeutic regimen are followed under careful physician supervision."[30]

As we saw in Chapter 2, this statement is blatantly false. It also does not conform to the approved professional labeling for Valium, which appeared (in very small print) at the end of each of these ads. Moreover, in the early version of this advertisement, the product labeling did not include the required statement advising against treatment of everyday stress with an anti-anxiety drug.

In June 1981, the Health Research Group wrote to Commissioner Arthur Hull Hayes of the Food and Drug Administration, asking the FDA to exercise its authority to prevent the publication of false or misleading drug advertising.[31]

After some discussion, Roche agreed to withdraw the objectionable language, and shortly thereafter decided to terminate the entire Talking Pill campaign.

But Roche had still not learned its lesson. Just a few months later, early in 1982, Dr. Sidney Wolfe, Director of the Public Citizen Health Research Group, called the FDA once more to complain about yet another false and misleading advertisement for Valium.

This advertisement, headlined "The Mind and Muscle

Action of Valium," depicted a human brain and muscle apparently streaking through space at the end of colored filaments. Here, Valium was presented as a drug for the treatment of muscular tension accompanying emotional tension—an indication for which the drug had never been approved.[32]

While Valium has been approved by the FDA for management of anxiety, as well as for use as an adjunct in treatment of muscle spasm caused by localized muscle disorders, it was not approved for the use stated in this advertisement. While this may appear to be a fine point, it serves as yet another example of Roche's frantic efforts to develop new markets for its product.

So blatant was this misstatement, in fact, that the telephone call from Dr. Wolfe to the FDA resulted in a promise that this advertising claim would be terminated.[33]

Valium is not the only tranquilizer of the benzodiazepine family promoted in medical journals or direct-mail advertising to physicians. Since it is the best-selling of these drugs, however, many of the advertisements for competing cousins have attempted to create a market by showing their product's superiority to Valium in specific ways. Implicit in all of these advertisements is the assumption that the physician will assuredly prescribe some kind of anti-anxiety drug.

Thus, Tranxene (clorazepate) claims that it avoids the "buzz" or a "high" that it attributes to Valium (diazepam)[34] or the "rebound" that it attributes to Ativan (lorazepam).[35] Illustrating these claims are softly colored photographs of an elegant woman's hands, one circled by gold bracelets and extinguishing a cigarette in a white china ashtray, the other perfectly manicured and cuffed in lace, counting out pills among expensive accessories.

Xanax (alprazolam) claims a favorable comparison with Valium (diazepam) in relieving anxiety.[36]

An ad for Ativan (lorazepam), on the other hand, claims the drug is superior to either Valium or Librium for use along with Tagamet, a best-selling prescription drug for ulcers. This advertisement, however, points out: "In patients where gastrointestinal disorders coexist with anxiety, it should be noted that benzodiazepines have not been shown to be of significant benefit in treating the gastrointestinal component."[37]

Nor has Valium a monopoly on fanciful advertising. An advertisement for Paxipam (halazepam) features a feathery white bird, which appears to be taking off from a metallic brain, promising "measurable peace of mind."[38]

Librium promises a winning number in the Bingo game of health.[39]

Restoril (temazepam) depicts an hourglass superimposed on a rosy dawn, along with happy, pajama-clad morning risers. This presumably reminds the reader of the manufacturer's claim that the product will not leave the patient drowsy in the morning.[40]

The advertisement for Dalmane (flurazepam), Roche's winner in the race for the benzodiazepine sleeping-pill sales crown, is perhaps one of the more "scientific"-looking benzodiazepine advertisements currently in print. It features the legend "Effective All Night" in bright blue neon letters over a green-and-yellow three-dimensional chart, depicting the product's claimed superiority over a field of nonbenzodiazepine sleeping products.[41]

Fantastic? This is what your doctor is reading every time he opens his medical journals, every time he looks at his mail.

Does it work? Would a multimillion-dollar industry keep on pouring money into this kind of promotion if it didn't?

The drug companies see to it that your doctor is

Feelings vs.

Some people feel that I am misused and overused and that I'm prescribed too often and for too many kinds of problems.

The FACT is that approximately eight million people, or about 5 percent of the U.S. adult population, will use me during the current year. By contrast, the national health examination survey (1971-1975) found that 25 percent of the U.S. adult population experiences moderate to severe psychological distress. Additionally, studies of patient attitudes revealed that most patients have realistic views regarding the limitations of tranquilizers and a strong conservatism about their use, as evidenced by a general tendency to *de*crease intake over time. Finally, a six-year, large-scale, carefully conducted national survey showed that the great majority of physicians appropriately prescribe tranquilizers.

Some people feel that patients being treated with anxiolytic drugs are "weak," can't tolerate the anxieties of normal daily living, and should be able to resolve their problems on their own without the help of medication.

The FACT is that while most people can withstand normal, everyday anxieties, some people experience excessive and persistent levels of anxiety due to personal or clinical problems. An extensive national survey concluded that Americans who do use tranquilizers have substantial

Facts

justification as evidenced by their high levels of anxiety. It was further noted that antianxiety drugs are not usually prescribed for trivial, transient emotional problems.

Some people feel afraid of me because of the stories they've heard about my being harmful and having the potential to produce physical dependence.

The FACT is that there are thousands of references in the medical literature documenting my efficacy and safety. Extensive and painstakingly thorough studies of toxicological data conclude that I am one of the safest types of psychotropic drugs available. Moreover, I do not cause physical dependence if the recommended dosage and therapeutic regimen are followed under careful physician supervision. However, I can produce dependence if patients do not follow their physicians' directions and take me for prolonged periods, at dosages that exceed the therapeutic range. Patients for whom I have been prescribed should be cautious about their use of alcohol because an additive effect may result.

Many of the most knowledgable people feel that I became the No. 1 prescribed medication in America because no other tranquilizer has been proven more effective. Or safer.

The FACT is they are right.

For a brief summary of product information on Valium (diazepam/Roche) ⒸIV, please see the following page. Valium is available as 2-mg, 5-mg and 10-mg scored tablets.

IF YOU'RE USING CLORAZEPATE TO TREAT ANXIETY— SOMETHING'S MISSING...
With Valium (diazepam/Roche)—two distinct actions, anxiety relief and skeletal muscle relaxation—to calm emotions and relax tense muscles.
Heightened emotional tension is accompanied by increased muscular tension in 65% of patients.[1] In a multicenter study, Valium demonstrated the ability to produce a statistically significant reduction in psychogenic muscular symptoms in 67 patients—even after just one week of treatment, with continuing improvement throughout four weeks of treatment.[2]
With Valium—a greater choice of dosage forms—three oral strengths plus I.M. and I.V.
With Valium—diazepam itself—working in concert with 3 active metabolites for the response you know and trust.
With Valium—an unmatched record of clinical experience and safety.
With all benzodiazepines—caution patients against drinking alcohol and against the immediate resumption of activities requiring complete mental alertness, such as driving.
References: 1. Clancy J, Noyes R Jr: Psychosomatics 17:90-93, April-June 1976. 2. Data on file, Medical Department, Hoffmann-La Roche Inc., Nutley, New Jersey 07110.

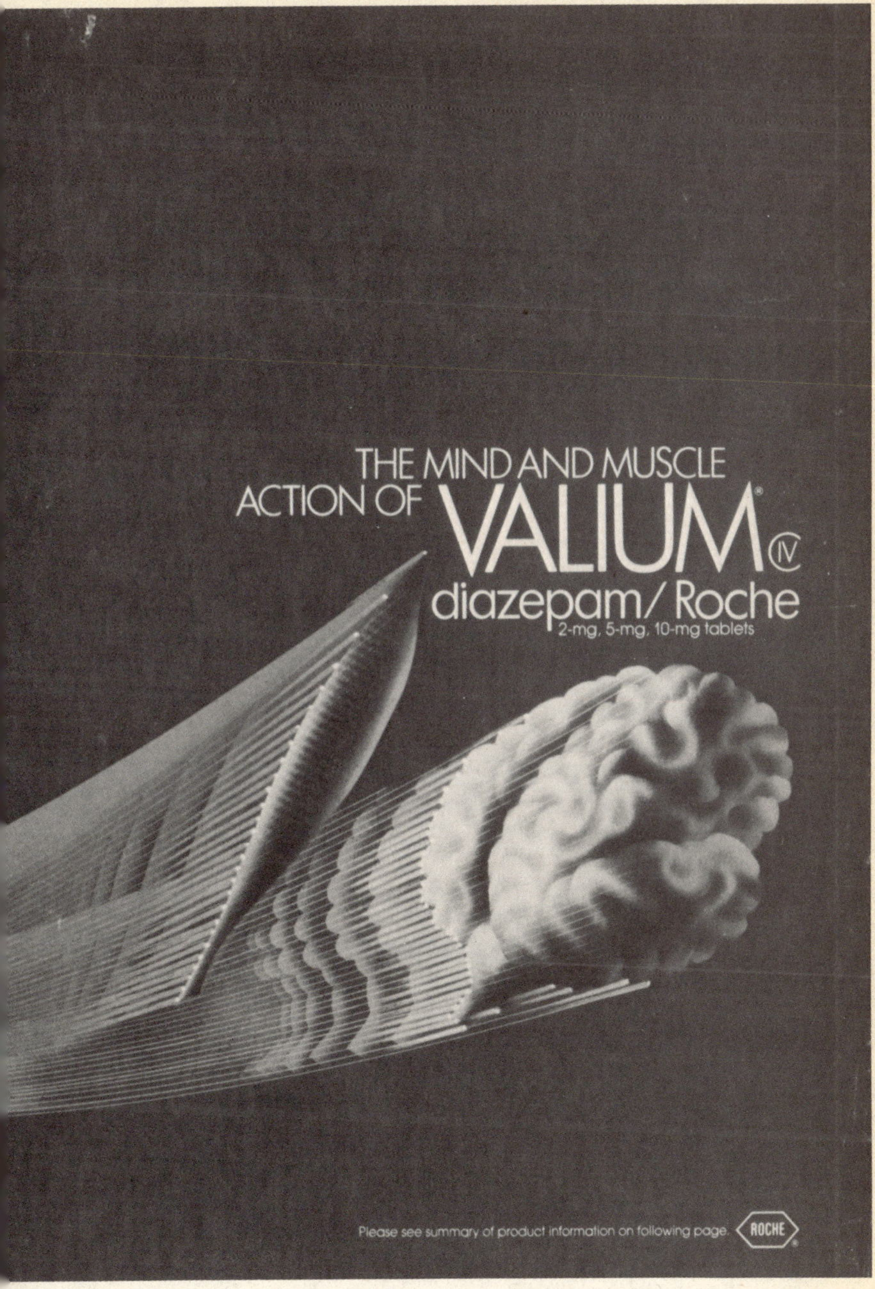
THE MIND AND MUSCLE
ACTION OF VALIUM® ⒸⅣ
diazepam/ Roche
2-mg, 5-mg, 10-mg tablets
Please see summary of product information on following page.
ROCHE

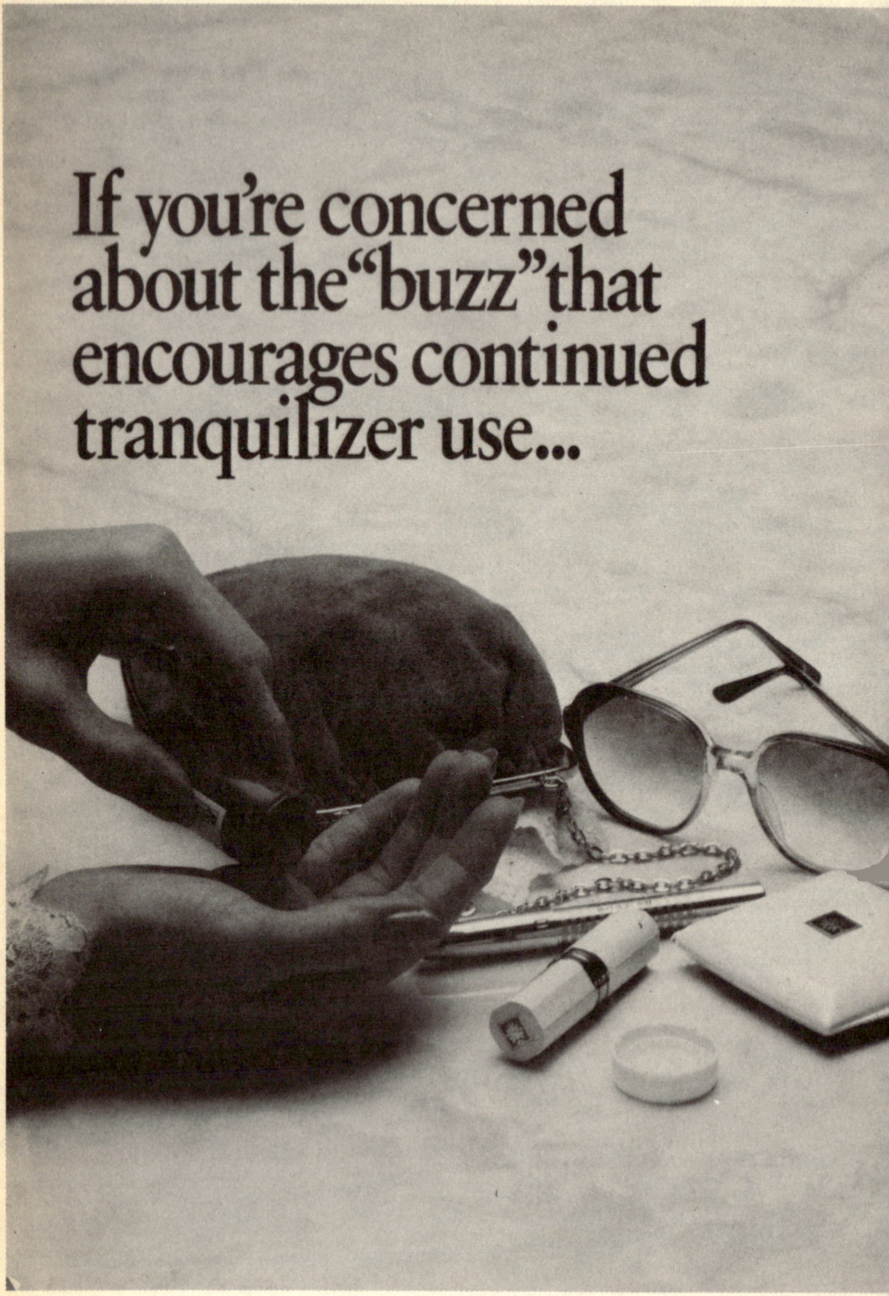
If you're concerned about the "buzz" that encourages continued tranquilizer use...

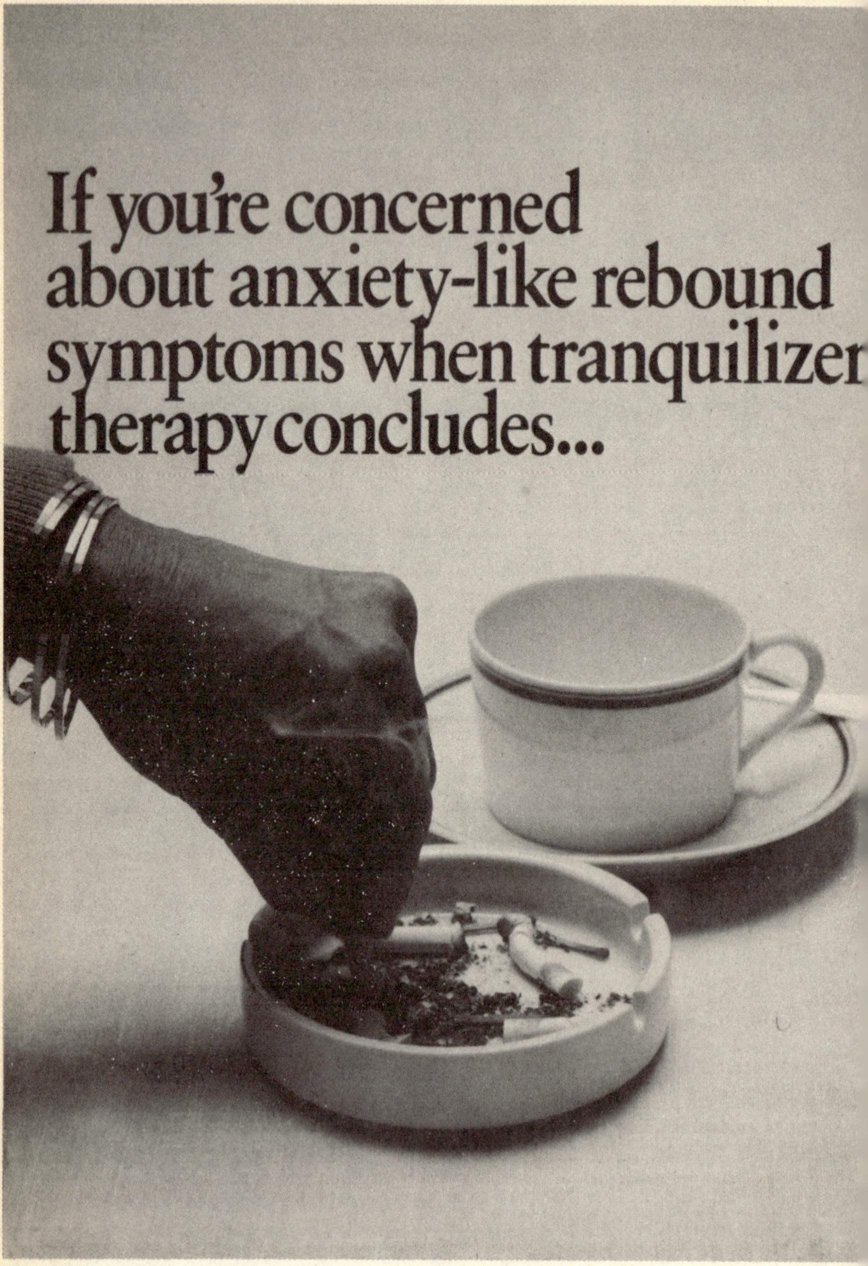
If you're concerned
about anxiety-like rebound
symptoms when tranquilizer
therapy concludes...

Tranxene® helps avoid them.

clorazepate dipotassium

4306CB

(C-IV)

Helps avoid effects that encourage drug-seeking behavior

Tranxene, a long-acting benzodiazepine, has a built-in tapering action.[1] There is no abrupt termination of pharmacologic effects. By contrast, a short-acting agent (like lorazepam) may cause anxiety-like rebound symptoms. These can encourage drug-seeking behavior and unwarranted readministration.[1,2]

Avoids drug-induced "buzz" or "high"

TRANXENE starts working promptly — yet with no reports of the initial euphoria that may be seen with the highly lipid-soluble agent diazepam.[3,4] This "buzz" effect, though transitory, may reinforce drug-taking behavior.[5,6]

Helps avoid disruptive effects of therapy

Eight years of clinical experience demonstrate that TRANXENE calms smoothly. It seldom causes problems due to oversedation and has a low incidence of significant side effects.

Tranxene is available as 3.75, 7.5, 15 mg capsules, scored tablets; 11.25, 22.5 mg single-dose tablets. For a brief summary of prescribing information, please see adjacent page.

NEW
Xanax 0.5 mg Tablets
CIV
FOR CLINICAL ANXIETY
EFFICACY CLEARLY COMPARABLE TO DIAZEPAM
WELL TOLERATED BY PATIENTS
RAPID ELIMINATION: EASY PERIODIC REASSESSMENT
USEFUL IN CLINICAL ANXIETY WITH ASSOCIATED DEPRESSIVE SYMPTOMATOLOGY
Upjohn
Please see next page for brief summary of prescribing information.

properly dazzled by some of the most brilliant minds in the advertising business.

But you are the person who will finally pay for the pills and swallow them, and you are the one who will suffer the consequences if they turn out to be harmful to you. For the sake of your health, be sure you (and your doctor) have the information you need to protect yourself against the hazards discussed in this book.

Your Doctor and the Drug Salesman—Behind Closed Doors

Fanciful, colorful, expensive advertisements carried in medical journals and delivered in the doctor's mail are only part of the massive drug-sales effort aimed at prescribing physicians from coast to coast.

Each day, thousands of drug-company salespeople, or detailmen, call on tens of thousands of physicians in their offices or at hospitals to promote their companies' products. In 1976, there were about 20,000 drug-company detailmen working in the United States.[42]

Over two-thirds of the total 1978 yearly advertising budget of 25 major drug companies in the United States was allotted to detailmen.[43]

The detailman is the foot soldier in the drug manufacturer's campaign to sell his drug to you. He visits the physician, he answers the questions, he makes suggestions, and he says what experience and careful training by his company have taught him the physician wants to hear. Above all, he does everything he can to make sure that the physicians in his territory prescribe his company's products.

How Tagamet does not affect the clearance of Ativan® (lorazepam) Ⓒ

"...pretreatment for 7 days with therapeutic doses of cimetidine does not impair the elimination of lorazepam...."[3]

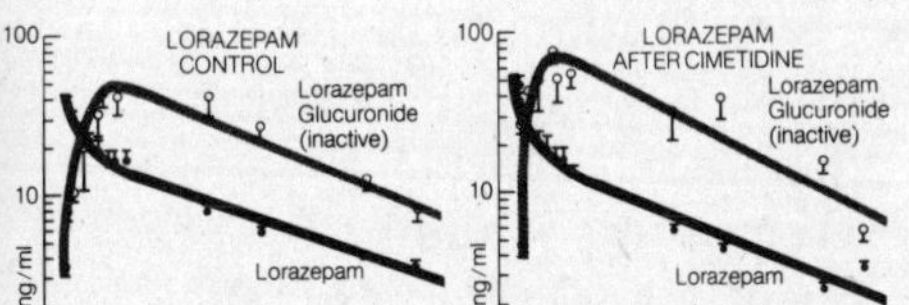

Plasma concentration/time profile for lorazepam and lorazepam glucuronide in 8 normal subjects on cimetidine 300 mg q.i.d. for 7 days before and throughout the 48 hours of the study. Lorazepam was given IV over one minute at a single dose of 2 mg. (Adapted from Patwardhan RV, Yarborough GW, Desmond PV, et al[3])

Ativan® (lorazepam) Ⓒ for Anxiety

References: 1. Klotz U, Reimann I: N Engl J Med *302*:1012-1014, 1980. **2.** Desmond PV, Patwardhan RV, Schenker S, et al: Ann Intern Med *93*:266-268, 1980. **3.** Patwardhan RV, Yarborough GW, Desmond PV, et al: Gastroenterology 79:912-916, 1980.

It is to the detailmen that your doctor may turn with questions about particular patient needs—perhaps your needs. While the detailman has been trained by his company, and may even have had college or graduate science courses, he is neither a doctor nor a pharmacologist. Yet he is the one who finally ties together the persuasive themes of the advertisements, by means of his personal, low-key sales pitch, and leaves your doctor feeling confident that the advertised drug is the right treatment for you.

Surveys have shown that the majority of physicians are favorably disposed toward detailmen, and that nearly half rely on them as a major source of information leading to the prescribing of new drugs.[44]

Although the detailman visits physicians unaccompanied, his performance is carefully monitored by the drug company he works for. Physicians are frequently asked to rate the detailman's performance and to name the drugs mentioned. The physician receives nothing for helping the drug company check up on the detailman, but the drug company may make a small contribution to a medical school named by the physician—a pleasant incentive for many doctors.[45]

Roche has long considered pushing Valium to be a top priority for detailmen's calls on physicians. The 1977 Western Region Plan called for sales staff to "continue to promote Valium on every call to objective physicians and in institutions."[46]

In 1979, the U.S. Senate Subcommittee on Health and Scientific Research of the Committee on Labor and Human Resources held a hearing on the Use and Misuse of Benzodiazepines.[47]

BINGO!
LOOKS LIKE MR. BROWN HAS THE WINNING COMBINATION.
HE SURE DOES. HIS CARDIOVASCULAR REGIMEN PLUS ADJUNCTIVE LIBRIUM® (chlordiazepoxide HCl/ROCHE) FOR HIS ANXIETY
WEBER

Because
the quality of awakening
is as important as
the quality of sleep...

Works one night at a time... from the first night

Highly effective

In 21 double-blind, placebo-controlled studies involving 1,221 adult patients (508 of whom received RESTORIL® capsules), RESTORIL (temazepam) proved to be an effective sleep agent.

The following advantages were noted:

- Therapeutically effective on the first night of therapy
- Significantly reduced number of nocturnal awakenings
- Effective total sleep time of 7 to 8 hours
- Significant improvement in general quality of sleep
- Residual medication effect essentially absent
- REM sleep remains essentially unchanged
- No tolerance reported to date after approximately one month of use (25 patients)

  Patients receiving RESTORIL (temazepam) should be cautioned about possible combined effects with alcohol and other CNS depressants, and about operating machinery or driving a vehicle after ingesting the drug.

An alert awakening... and an alert patient

Because of the short half-life of RESTORIL (temazepam) there is minimal accumulation of drug in the body, leaving the patient essentially free of drug effect and showing little or no impairment of behavior in the morning. In placebo-controlled studies, patients receiving RESTORIL capsules reported being at least as awake in the morning and as alert the following day as did the patients who received placebo.

Useful for most adult insomniacs

RESTORIL (temazepam) has been used effectively in adult and elderly patients* with recurring insomnia, and in situations requiring restful sleep.

*Recommended initial dose for elderly patients is one 15 mg capsule.

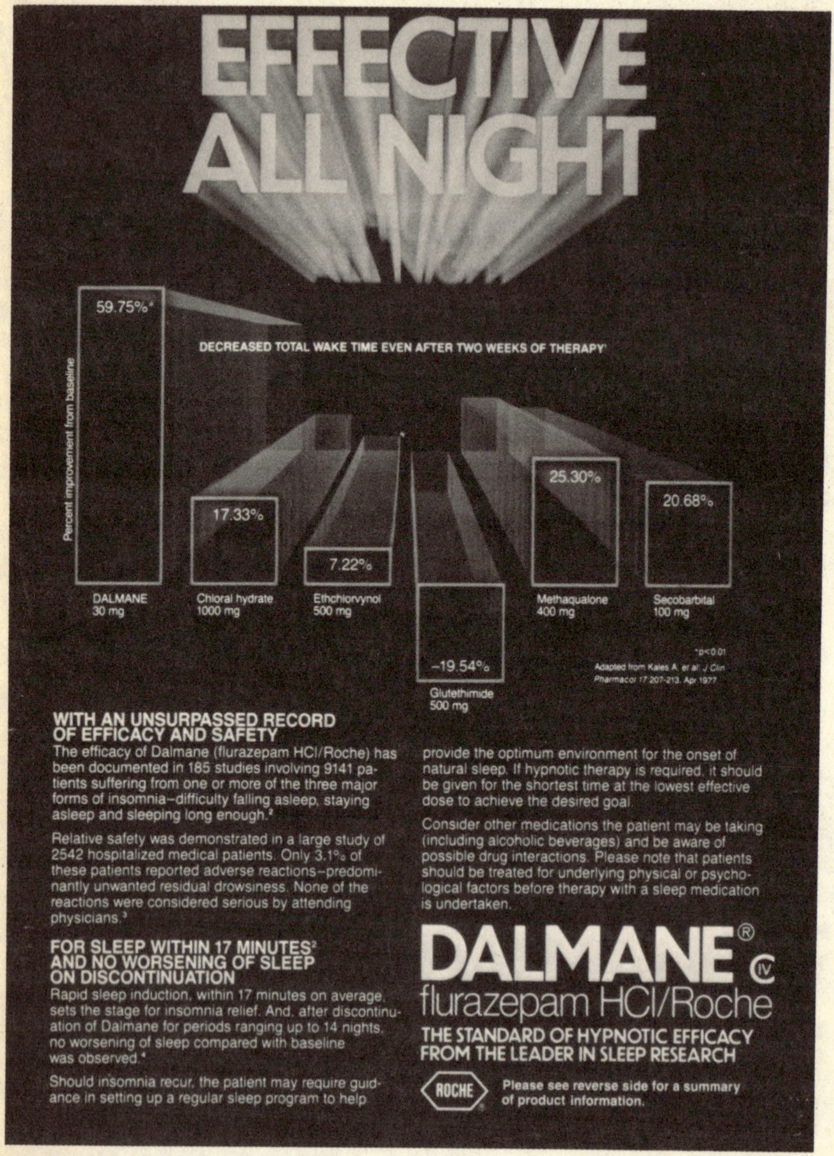
EFFECTIVE ALL NIGHT
59.75%*
DECREASED TOTAL WAKE TIME EVEN AFTER TWO WEEKS OF THERAPY[1]
Percent improvement from baseline
17.33%
7.22%
25.30%
20.68%
–19.54%
DALMANE 30 mg
Chloral hydrate 1000 mg
Ethchlorvynol 500 mg
Glutethimide 500 mg
Methaqualone 400 mg
Secobarbital 100 mg
*p<0.01
Adapted from Kales A, et al: J Clin Pharmacol 17:207-213, Apr 1977
WITH AN UNSURPASSED RECORD OF EFFICACY AND SAFETY
The efficacy of Dalmane (flurazepam HCl/Roche) has been documented in 185 studies involving 9141 patients suffering from one or more of the three major forms of insomnia–difficulty falling asleep, staying asleep and sleeping long enough.[2]
Relative safety was demonstrated in a large study of 2542 hospitalized medical patients. Only 3.1% of these patients reported adverse reactions–predominantly unwanted residual drowsiness. None of the reactions were considered serious by attending physicians.[3]
FOR SLEEP WITHIN 17 MINUTES[2] AND NO WORSENING OF SLEEP ON DISCONTINUATION
Rapid sleep induction, within 17 minutes on average, sets the stage for insomnia relief. And, after discontinuation of Dalmane for periods ranging up to 14 nights, no worsening of sleep compared with baseline was observed.[4]
Should insomnia recur, the patient may require guidance in setting up a regular sleep program to help provide the optimum environment for the onset of natural sleep. If hypnotic therapy is required, it should be given for the shortest time at the lowest effective dose to achieve the desired goal.
Consider other medications the patient may be taking (including alcoholic beverages) and be aware of possible drug interactions. Please note that patients should be treated for underlying physical or psychological factors before therapy with a sleep medication is undertaken.
DALMANE® CIV
flurazepam HCl/Roche
THE STANDARD OF HYPNOTIC EFFICACY FROM THE LEADER IN SLEEP RESEARCH
ROCHE
Please see reverse side for a summary of product information.

At this hearing, Senator Edward M. Kennedy pointed out that in 1977 a telegram went from a field sales manager to detailmen saying:

> *The southern area has a good share of the market, but Valium new prescriptions are flat and new competition is imminent. Let's get on with the strategy of Valium number one on all calls now to keep what we've got and to assure the necessary growth in 1977. Please send a written note indicating to your regional manager by December 17 your understanding of this directive and your commitment to Valium on every call.*[48]

Since Valium and Librium accounted for nearly half of Roche's United States sales at this time,[49] such directives were hardly surprising. Senator Kennedy interpreted this as "pressure on [Roche's] sales force to reverse the decline of sales that began when Valium was made a scheduled drug and a controlled substance."[50]

What does all this mean to you? It means that when your doctor opens the office door to the pleasant young man or woman who is eager to help, listen to, and even advise your doctor, your doctor is being influenced in favor of a particular line of drugs. This is important to you, because when the detailman is in the office alone with your doctor, away from the eyes and ears of the FDA, you can be quite certain that he is often not sharing with your doctor important information about addiction and the other hazards of Valium and its cousins.

The backbone of drug advertisement is journal advertising, direct-mail advertising, and detailmen. However, the major drug companies make their names and products known in other ways as well.

Along with gifts to medical students, which have been discussed, drug companies sponsor exhibits at medical-society meetings, organize entire conferences on specific medical subjects, participate in continuing medical-education programs for physicians, advertise on Physicians Radio Network (a limited-access wavelength featuring informational programs for doctors) and closed-circuit educational television, display "public information" advertising, and generally try to keep their names and products in the public and professional eye in as favorable a light as possible.

Today, there are few sources of medical information available to practicing physicians that are not funded, wholly or in significant part, by the drug industry.

Patient—Beware!

In a 1976 article in the *Journal of Drug Issues,* former United States Senator Gaylord Nelson summed up years of hearings by the Monopoly Subcommittee of the Senate Small Business Committee by noting "irrefutable evidence that the system of marketing drugs in this country is deleterious to the interests of the public."[51]

Senator Nelson stated:

> A principal cause of . . . misuse [of drugs] is that many prescribing physicians depend largely on the industry for their information about drugs. The prescription drug industry in 1971 spent more than $1 billion on advertising and promotion . . . In my judgment, drug advertising by its very nature cannot provide unbiased information to physicians . . .[52]

As former FDA Commissioner Charles C. Edwards explained to Senator Nelson's subcommittee in 1971:

> The advertising industry took advantage of . . . the increasing complexity of our society and the discovery of the mood drugs to promote and advertise these drugs in such a way as to actually create a climate of need . . . A casual examination of the medical journals indicates that prescription mood drugs are being promoted at such rates and with such themes as to create an unrealistic demand for these drugs. In other words, the manufacturers of prescription psychotherapeutic drugs are stretching the uses and the intent of the medications beyond their proven medical benefits. The general tenor of these advertisements is cleverly designed to create an unnecessary demand for the drug.[53]

Senator Nelson called for a way to insure that physicians receive adequate and objective information in order to select the best treatment for patients, without the biased interference of the drug industry.

Unfortunately, we are no closer to Senator Nelson's goal today than we were in 1976.

It is up to you, therefore, to practice intelligent, well-informed, defensive consumerism. Your health—and perhaps your life—may depend on it.

References

Chapter 1

1. Burke, L., et al. *Benzodiazepines: Extent and Character of Use.* U.S. Food and Drug Administration, October 18, 1979.

2. Drug Abuse Warning Network. *1980 DAWN Annual Report.* DEA Contract #81-3. U.S. Drug Enforcement Administration, 1981.

3. National Institute on Drug Abuse. *1980 Data from the Client Oriented Data Acquisition Process.* Series E, #21. U.S. Department of Health and Human Services, July 1981.

4. Committee on the Review of Medicines. "Systematic review of the benzodiazepines." *Brit. Med. J.* 1980; 1:910–912.

5. "Choice of benzodiazepines." *The Medical Letter.* 1981; 23:41–43.

6. Wittenborn, J.R. "Effects of benzodiazepines on psychomotor performance." *Brit. J. Clin. Pharmacol.* 1979; 7:61S–67S.

7. Hindmarch, I., et al. "The effects of clobazam and lorazepam on aspects of psychomotor performance and car handling ability." *Brit. J. Clin. Pharmacol.* 1980; 10:145–150.

8. Skegg, D.C.G., et al. "Minor tranquillisers and road accidents." *Brit. Med. J.* 1979; 1:917–919.

9. "Drugs that cause psychiatric symptoms." *The Medical Letter.* 1981; 23:9–12.

10. Drug Abuse Warning Network, op. cit.

11. National Prescription Audit, 1980. IMS America, Ambler, PA.

12. Ibid.

13. Hoffmann-LaRoche. Advertisement for Librium. *J. Amer. Coll. Health Assoc.,* June 1969.

14. Waldron, I. "Increased prescribing of Valium, Librium, and other drugs—an example of the influence of economic and social factors on the practice of medicine." *Int. J. Health Serv.* 1977; 7 (1).

15. Hoffmann-LaRoche. Advertisement for Valium, received by Sidney M. Wolfe, M.D., Jan. 6, 1982.

16. Burke et al., op. cit.

17. Huxley, A. *Brave New World Revisited.* New York: Harper & Row, 1960, p. 61.

18. Solomon, K. "Benzodiazepines and neurotic anxiety." *New York State J. Med.* 1976; 176:2156–2164.

19. Louria, D. B. Statement before the U.S. Senate Subcommittee on Monopoly. Advertising of Proprietary Medicines, Part 2, July 21–23, 1971, p. 510.

20. National Prescription Audit, op. cit.

Chapter 2

1. Use and Misuse of Benzodiazepines: Hearing on Examination on the Use and Misuse of Valium, Librium, and other Minor Tranquilizers Before the Subcommittee on Health and Scientific Research of the Senate Committee on Labor and Human Resources, 96th Congress, 1st Session, p. 11 (September 10, 1979).

2. Ibid., p. 14.

3. World Health Organization Expert Committee on Drug Dependence, 16th report. WHO Tech. Rep. Series, 1969, p. 407.

4. Burke, L., et al. "Benzodiazepines: Extent and Character of Use." Unpublished draft. U.S. Food and Drug Administration. October 18, 1979.

5. Levine, J. Statement before the Senate Subcommittee on Monopoly. Quoted in *FDC Reports,* July 21, 1969, p. 7.

6. Tyrer, P., et al. "Benzodiazepine withdrawal symptoms and propranolol." *Lancet.* 1981; 1:520–522.

7. Maletzky, B.M., and Klotter, J. "Addiction to diazepam." *Int. J. Addictions.* 1976; 11:95–115.

8. Petursson, H., and Lader, M.H. "Withdrawal from long-term benzodiazepine treatment." *Brit. Med. J.* 1981; 283: 643–645.

9. "Choice of benzodiazepines." *The Medical Letter.* 1981; 23:41–43.

10. Covi, L., et al. "Length of treatment with anxiolytic sedatives and response to their sudden withdrawal." *Acta Psychiatr. Scand.* 1973; 49:51–64.

11. Rifkin, A., et al. "Withdrawal reaction to diazepam." *J. Am. Med. Assoc.* 1976; 236:2172–2173.

12. Use and Misuse of Benzodiazepines, op. cit., p. 5.

13. Synder, S.H. *Biological Aspects of Mental Disorder.* New York: Oxford University Press, 1980. Cited in Ayd, F.J. "Diazepam dependency and withdrawal." *Current Psychiatric Therapies: 1981;* p. 270.

14. "Choice of benzodiazepines," op. cit.

15. Maletzky and Klotter, op cit.

16. Tyrer, et al., op. cit.

17. Ibid.

18. Rifkin, et al., op. cit.

19. Minter, R., and Murray G.B. "Diazepam withdrawal: A current problem in recognition. *J. Fam. Practice.* 1978; 7:1233–1235.

20. Use and Misuse of Benzodiazepines, op. cit., pp. 299–325. Statement by Robert B. Clark.

21. Use and Misuse of Benzodiazepines, op. cit., p. 167.

22. Marks, J. *The Benzodiazepines: Use, Overuse, Misuse, Abuse.* Lancaster, England: MTP Press, 1978.

23. White, O.Z., et al. "A Report on the Prescribing of Minor Tranquilizers in Texas." Texas Medical Association, 1980.

24. Drug Abuse Warning Network. *1980 DAWN Annual Report.* U.S. Drug Enforcement Administration, DEA Contract #81–3, 1981.

25. Ibid.

26. National Institute on Drug Abuse. 1979 Data from the Client Oriented Data Acquisition Process. Series E, #17. U.S. Department of Health and Human Services, 1980.

27. National Institute on Drug Abuse. 1980 Data from the Client Oriented Data Acquisition Process. Series E, #21. U.S. Department of Health and Human Services, 1981.

28. Burke, et al., op. cit.

29. Ibid.

30. Use and Misuse of Benzodiazepines, op. cit., pp. 299–325. Statement by Robert B. Clark.

31. Maletzky and Klotter, op. cit.

32. Ibid.

33. National Institute on Drug Abuse. 1980 Data from the Client Oriented Data Acquisition Process, op. cit.

Chapter 3

1. Davies, D.M. *Textbook of Adverse Drug Reactions.* Oxford, England: Oxford University Press, 1977, p. 337. And see: The Upjohn Company. Data on clinical trial comparing diazepam and alprazolam for the treatment of depression. Presented to FDA's Psychopharmacologic Drugs Advisory Committee Meeting, June 10, 1982.

2. Wittenborn, J.R. "Effects of benzodiazepines on psychomotor performance." *Brit. J. Clin. Pharmacol.* 1979; 7:615–675.

3. Morland, J., et al. "Combined effects of diazepam and alcohol on mental and psychomotor functions." *Acta Pharmacol. et Toxicol.* 1974; 34:5–15.

4. Hindmarch, I., and Gudgeon, A.C. "The effects of clobazam and lorazepam on aspects of psychomotor performance and car handling ability." *Brit. J. Clin. Pharmacol.* 1980; 10:145–150. This study was done in Europe, using lorazepam. Lorazepam is sold in this country as Ativan.

5. Drug Abuse Warning Network. *1980 DAWN Annual Report.* DEA Contract #81-3. U.S. Drug Enforcement Administration, 1981.

6. "Drugs that cause psychiatric symptoms." *The Medical Letter.* 1981; 23:9–12.

7. "Choice of benzodiazepines." *The Medical Letter.* 1981; 23:41–43.

8. Milkovich, L., and van den Berg, B.J. "Effects of prenatal meprobamate and chlordiazepoxide hydrochloride on human embryonic and fetal development." *New Eng. J. Med.* 1974; 291:1268–1271.

9. Drug Abuse Warning Network, op. cit.

10. Ibid.

11. Ibid.

12. National Prescription Audit. Ambler, Pa: IMS America, 1978, 1979, 1980.

13. Burke, L., et al. "Benzodiazepines: Extent and Character of Use," unpublished U.S. Food and Drug Administration, October 18, 1979.

14. Drug Abuse Warning Network, op. cit.

15. Ibid.

16. Ibid.

17. Ibid.

18. Drug Abuse Warning Network Data. Reproduced in Use and Misuse of Benzodiazepines. Hearing before the Senate Subcommittee on Health and Scientific Research, September 10, 1979, pp. 476–484.

19. Cooperstock, R., Lennard, H., and Vayda, E. "Problems Associated with Benzodiazepine Use in Canada," unpublished. March 20, 1978, p. 15.

20. Guile, L.A. "Rapid habituation to chlordiazepoxide." *Med. J. Aust.* 1963; 2:56–57.

21. Use and Misuse of Benzodiazepines, op. cit. Statement by N. Hendler, pp. 23–25.

22. Cassone, M.C., and Molinengo, L. "Action of thyroid hormones, diazepam, caffeine, and amitriptyline on memory decay (forgetting)." *Life Sciences.* 1981; 29:1983–1988.

23. Davies, op. cit., p. 337.

24. Greenblatt, D.J., and Shader, R.I. "Benzodiazepines." *New Eng. J. Med.* 1974; 291:1239–1243.

25. Wittenborn, op. cit.

26. Morland, op. cit.

27. McKay, A.C., and Dundee, J.W. "Effect of oral benzodiazepines on memory." *Brit. J. Anaesth.* 1980; 52:1247–1256.

28. Wittenborn, op. cit.

29. Ibid.

30. Gottschalk, L.A. "Effects of certain benzodiazepine derivatives on disorganization of thought as manifested in speech." *Curr. Ther. Res.* 1977; 21:192–206.

31. "Drugs that cause psychiatric symptoms," op. cit.

32. Ibid.

33. Greenblatt, op. cit.

34. Use and Misuse of Benzodiazepines, op. cit.

35. Betts, T.A., et al. "Effects of four commonly-used tranquillisers on low-speed driving performance." *Brit. Med. J.* 1972; 4:580–584.

36. Hindmarch and Gudgeon, op. cit.

37. Skegg, D.C.G. "Minor tranquillisers and road accidents." *Brit. Med. J.* 1979; 1:917–919.

38. Morland, op. cit.

39. Hindmarch, I. "Benzodiazepines and traffic accidents." *Brit. Med. J.* 1979; 2:671.

40. Wittenborn, op. cit.

41. Hindmarch, op. cit.

42. Linnoila, M., and Mattila, M.J. "Drug interaction on psychomotor skills related to driving: diazepam and alcohol." *Eur. J. Clin. Pharmacol.* 1973; 5:186–194.

43. Morland, op. cit.

44. Saxen, I. "Associations between oral clefts and drugs taken during pregnancy." *Int. J. Epidemiol.* 1975; 4:37–44.

45. Safra, M.J., and Oakley, G.P. "Association between cleft lip with or without cleft palate and prenatal exposure to diazepam." *Lancet.* 1975; 2:478–480.

46. Milkovich and van den Berg, op. cit.

47. Hartz, S.C., et al. "Antenatal exposure to meprobamate and chlordiazepoxide in relation to malformations, mental development, and childhood mortality." *New Eng. J. Med.* 1982; 292:726–728.

48. "Teratogenicity of minor tranquilizers." *FDA Drug Bulletin.* September–November 1975, pp. 14–15.

49. Speight, A.N.P. "Floppy-infant syndrome and maternal diazepam and/or nitrazepam." *Lancet.* 1977; 2:878.

50. Rowlatt, R.J. "Effect of maternal diazepam on the newborn." *Brit. Med. J.* 1978; 1:985.

51. Finnegan, L. Testimony before the Select Committee on Narcotics Abuse and Control, U.S. House of Representatives, Ninety-sixth Congress, Second Session, February 6, 1980, pp. 29–39. Quoted in *FDC Reports.* February 11, 1980, pp. T&G–14.

52. Rowlatt, op. cit.

53. Boston Collaborative Drug Surveillance Program. "Clinical depression of the central nervous system due to diazepam and chlordiazepoxide in relation to cigarette smoking and age." *New Eng. J. Med.* 1973; 288:277–280.

54. Committee on the Review of Medicines. "Systematic review of the benzodiazepines." *Brit. Med. J.* 1980; 280:910–912.

55. Ramsay, L.E., and Tucker, G.T. "Clinical pharmacology: Drugs and the elderly." *Brit. Med. J.* 1981; 282:125–127.

56. Dement, W. Presentation before the Joint Coordinating Council for Project Sleep. July 28, 1980.

57. Hoffmann-LaRoche. Prescribing information for Valium. August 1, 1981.

58. Ibid.

59. Lakshminarayan, S., et al. "Effect of diazepam on ventilatory responses." *Clin. Pharm. Ther.* 1976; 20:178–183.

60. Ghosh, J.S. "Allergy to diazepam and other benzodiazepines." *Brit. Med. J.* 1977: 1:902–903.

61. Hyams, S.W., and Keroub, C. "Glaucoma due to diazepam." *Am. J. Psychiatry.* 1977; 134:447–448.

62. Hoffmann-LaRoche, op. cit.

63. Bergman, D., et al. Increased estradiol in diazepam related gynaecomastia." *Lancet.* 1981; 2:1225–1226.

64. Kaplan, S.R., and Murkofsky, C. "Oral-buccal dyskinesia syndrome associated with low-dose benzodiazepine treatment." *Am. J. Psychiatry.* 1978; 135:1558–1559.

65. Fox, K.A., and Lahcen, R.B. "Liver-cell adenomas and peliosis hepatis in mice associated with oxazepam." *Res. Comm. Chem. Path. Pharmacol.* 1974; 8:481–488.

66. Rosenbaum, J.F. "The drug treatment of anxiety." *New Eng. J. Med.* 1982; 306:401–404.

67. Hoffmann-LaRoche, op. cit.

68. Desmond, P.V. "Cimetidine impairs elimination of chlordiazepoxide (Librium) in man." *Ann. Int. Med.* 1980; 93:266–268.

69. Dukes, M.N.G. *Side Effects of Drugs Annual 4.* Princeton: Excerpta Medica, 1980, p. 352.

70. American Pharmaceutical Association. *Evaluation of Drug Interactions,* 2nd ed. Washington, D.C.: American Pharmaceutical Association, 1976, p. 124.

71. Abernethy, D.R., et al. "Impairment of diazepam metabolism by low-dose estrogen-containing oral-contraceptive steroids." *New Eng. J. Med.* 1982; 306:791–792.

72. Food and Drug Administration. Patient Package Inserts Requirements. 45 Fed. Reg. 60754–60817, September 12, 1980.

73. Ibid.

Chapter 4

1. Competitive Problems in the Drug Industry: Hearings Before the Subcommittee on Monopoly of the Select Committee on Small Business, U.S. Senate, Ninety-second Congress, Second Session, July 16, 1969. Part 13, p. 5290.

2. Distilled Spirits Industry: Annual Statistical Review, 1974. Distilled Spirits Council of the United States, p. 43.

3. National Prescription Audit. Ambler, Pa.: IMS America, 1975, 1980.

4. Zung, W.W.K., Daniel, J.T., King, R.E., and Moore, D.T. "A comparison of prazepam, diazepam, lorazepam, and placebo in anxious outpatients in non-psychiatric private practices." *J. Clin. Psychiatry.* 1981; 42:280–284.

5. Skegg, D.C.G. "Minor tranquillisers and road accidents." *Brit. Med. J.* 1979; 1:917–919.

6. Hoffmann-LaRoche. Prescribing information for Valium. August 1, 1981.

7. Ibid.

8. Ibid.

9. Desmond, P.V. "Cimetidine impairs elimination of chlordiazepoxide (Librium) in man." *Ann. Int. Med.* 1980; 93:266–268.

10. Dukes, M.N.G. *Side Effects of Drugs Annual 4.* Princeton: Excerpta Medica, 1980, p. 352.

11. Abernethy, D.R., et al. "Impairment of diazepam metabolism by low-dose estrogen-containing oral-contraceptive steroids." *New Eng. J. Med.* 1982; 306:791–792.

12. American Pharmaceutical Association. *Evaluation of Drug Interactions,* 2nd ed. Washington, D.C.: American Pharmaceutical Association, 1976, p. 124.

Chapter 5

1. Covi, L., et al. Factors affecting withdrawal response to certain minor tranquilizers. In Cole, J.O., and Wittenborn, J.R. (eds.), *Drug Abuse: Social and Psychopharmacological Aspects.* Springfield, Ill.: Charles C. Thomas Pub., 1969, pp. 93–108.

2. National Institute on Drug Abuse. 1980 Data from the Client Oriented Data Acquisition Process. Series E, #21. U.S. Department of Health and Human Services, 1981.

3. Drug Abuse Warning Network. *1980 DAWN Annual Report.* U.S. Drug Enforcement Administration, DEA Contract #81-3, 1981.

4. Khan, A., et al. "Benzodiazepine withdrawal syndromes." *N.Z. Med. J.* 1980; 92:94–96.

Chapter 6

1. *Medical World News,* December 21, 1981.

2. *Physician's Management,* February 1982.

3. Mailing to physicians, 1981.

4. *Advertising Age,* November 5, 1979, S-5, 6.

5. Conversation with Linda Rabinowitz, M.D. Dr. Rabinowitz was a fourth-year student at Harvard Medical School when this book was written.

6. Ibid.

7. *Chicago Sun Times,* Friday, January 17, 1975, pp. 4, 16.

8. Shansky, R., et al. "Licit Drugs: The problem and an initial effort aimed at a solution." December 1976. Unpublished manuscript.

9. Advertising of Proprietary Medicines: Hearings before the Subcommittee on Monopoly of the Senate Select Committee on Small Business, 92nd Congress, 1st Session. Effect of Promotion and Advertising of Over-the-

Counter Drugs on Competition, Small Business and the Health and Welfare of the Public. Part 2 (Sedatives, Tranquilizers and Stimulants), 1971, p. 546 (hereinafter cited as 1971 Senate Hearings).

10. Ibid., pp. 824–825.

11. Ibid.

12. Ibid., pp. 868–869.

13. Ibid., pp. 842–843.

14. Ibid., pp. 840–841.

15. Ibid., pp. 856–857.

16. Mailings to physicians, 1979.

17. Ibid.

18. Mailing to physicians, "The later years . . . an optimistic outlook," 1979.

19. Mailing to physicians, "Stress and the Senior Citizen . . ." 1979.

20. Mailing to physicians, "Roche Seminars on Aging," 1982.

21. Edwards, C.C. Letter to sponsors. FDA, October 22, 1971.

22. *FDA Drug Bulletin.* November 1980; 10:23.

23. Mailing to physicians, "Negative Tests, Positive Symptoms," 1981.

24. Mailing to physicians, 1975.

25. Mailing to physicians, 1981.

26. "Sedative-Hypnotic Drugs: Risks and Benefits." U.S. Department of Health and Human Services; Public Health Service; Alcohol, Drug Abuse and Mental Health Administration. November 1977.

27. Memorandum of Meeting, April 9, 1979 prepared by Kenneth R. Feather, Consumer Safety Officer, Division of Drug Advertising, FDA, regarding meeting with Hoffmann-LaRoche on the subject "Use of NIDA Report 'Sedative-Hypnotic Drugs: Risks and Benefits' by Roche, our letter of January 25, 1979 and March 5, 1979"; NDA-263.

28. Mailing to physicians, "Valium (diazepam) adjunctively," 1976.

29. Mailing to physicians, "In the anxious, post M-I patient," 1979.

30. *Medical World News,* May 11, 1981; *Drug Topics,* May 15, 1981 and June 5, 1981.

31. Letter from Sidney M. Wolfe, M.D., and Joan Levin to Arthur Hull Hayes, Jr., M.D., Commissioner, Food and Drug Administration, June 18, 1981.

32. *Medical World News,* December 21, 1981.

33. Telephone conversation between Sidney M. Wolfe, M.D., and Peter Rheinstein, M.D., former director of Drug Advertising and Labeling, FDA, January, 1982.

34. *Medical Economics,* February 15, 1982.

35. *Physician's Management,* February 1982.

36. *Medical Economics,* February 15, 1982.

37. Mailing to physicians, "Why Risk Oversedation?" 1981.

38. *Medical World News,* December 21, 1981.

39. *American Family Physician,* February 1982.

40. *Medical World News,* July 6, 1981.

41. *Medical World News,* November 9, 1981.

42. Hughes, R., and Brewin, R. *The Tranquilizing of America: Pill Popping and the American Way of Life.* New York: Harcourt Brace Jovanovich, 1979, p. 197.

43. *Advertising Age,* op. cit.

44. Miller, R.R. "Prescribing habits of physicians." *Drug Intelligence and Clinical Pharmacy.* 1974; 8:81–91.

45. Hughes and Brewin, op. cit., p. 206.

46. Use and Misuse of Benzodiazepines, op. cit., p. 173.

47. Ibid.

48. Ibid., pp. 179, 203.

49. *Advertising Age,* op. cit.

50. Use and Misuse of Benzodiazepines, op. cit., p. 203.

51. Nelson, G. "Advertising and the National Health." *Journal of Drug Issues.* 1976; 67:28–33.

52. Ibid., p. 28.

53. Ibid., p. 29.